Vegetarian Soul Food

A collection of 152 recipes
to nourish the body,
inspire the spirit,
and feed the soul.

From Karen S. Bard
to you.

Published by Karen S. Bard
181 Jericho Rd.
Pomfret Center, CT 06259

All poetry, prose, recipes and drawings by Karen Bard.

Excerpts by Wendell Berry, William Carlos Williams, Joyce Carol Oates, and Charles Simic from *Anteaeus: Not For Bread Alone*, published by the Ecco Press, Hopewell, NJ.
Excerpt by Isabelle Allende from *Aphrodite*, published by Harper Perennial, NY, NY.
Excerpt by Bernard Glassman from *Instructions to the Cook*. Reprinted by permission of Bell Tower, an imprint of Harmony Books, a division of Crown Publishers, NY, NY.
Excerpt by Thich Nhat Hanh from *Anger*. Reprinted by permission of Riverhead Books, a member of Penguin Putnam Inc., NY NY.

Layout by Steve Scanlon at Skeeter Studio
amosquito@earthlink.net

Printed by Signature Book Printing, Inc.
8041 Cessna Avenue, Suite 132
Gaithersburg, MD 20879

Printed on recycled paper.

I dedicate this book
to my mother, Annie
and my father, Elliot

May peace prevail on earth.

Contents

FAITH

...all things are less than
they are,
all are more...
-Paul Celan

Consider the seed.
Consider the flower containing the seed.
Consider the stem, that shy messenger,
carrying the secrets
of the underworld into the daylight.
Consider the root, fingering its way down, intimate
with the stones, the amazed dirt-
consider the seed, the stem
within the seed, the root
within the the seed, the flower
within the seed.
Consider your left palm,
warm, familiar, cupped
around a handful of seeds.
Consider your faith.

O wonderful! O wonderful! O wonderful!
I am food! I am food! I am food!
I eat food! I eat food! I eat food!
-Teittriya Upanishad

*W*e are all connected. You to me, to the stars, to the sun, to the trees and the bugs and the fishes and the four-leggeds and the two-leggeds. All of us here on this planet who have hearts, we eat. The dragonflies and the chickens and the goldfish, the mosquitoes and the owls and the iguanas, we eat. Preferably every day. Preferably more than once during that day. When we cannot eat, nothing else matters until we can eat again. This is as true for starfish and horses as it is for you and me. It's that simple.

You and me, though, with our human heads, hands, and bellies, we complicate things. We complicate things because that's our job. We are human and so we are given choices. The world is full of possibilities, not only of what we can do, but how we can do it. We can choose to look at the complexity and intricacy and subtlety of a thing, and be in awe of it. We can look at the same thing and be overwhelmed by it. We can hate it, we can love it. When we have gone through our feelings towards that thing, if we really look at it with all the awareness we can muster, it becomes very simple. We see that a part of us lives in that thing, and part of that thing lives in us. We are connected.

For me, my relationship to food-how it looks, how it feels, how can I grow it, how can I prepare it- has been my spiritual path. I didn't know this when my Hungarian mother taught me to make the dishes of her childhood. I didn't know this when I became anorexic and food (or the lack thereof) turned into an obsession. I didn't know this when people started to ask me to cook for them, for this retreat or that dinner party, for this wedding or that picnic. All I knew was that I loved to cook, and that people loved to eat. I didn't choose cooking as a way of life. Cooking chose me. I am so grateful that this way of making a living, being a gardener and a cook, is also my way of being close to the universal spirit, which lives in you. Which lives in egg-plants and spinach and rice and and bumblebees and dirt.

I have fed thousands of people in my journey as a cook. Most of them want recipes. Here they are. You will see that I do not engage in culinary wizardry. I also don't follow or write down recipes (though I find cookbooks inspirational), so writing this book has been a challenge. These recipes are merely guidelines. They are not "rules". Follow your heart when you follow a recipe. Pay attention. Pay attention. When you cook, just cook. Sounds easy. It's not. But worth the effort. With practice, it will become easy. When I am distracted, I mess up. I burn the cookies, I overcook the noodles. And then I laugh, am grateful that I didn't mess up worse than I did, and try again. It's an opportunity to exercise patience with myself. Everything is fine, it really is. I just try to put in that one ingredient, that one essential ingredient, that all great foods have: love. Put in some love, and dinner will be fabulous.

So, go forth- knife, cutting board, and onion in hand, and chop away! Smile! You have my blessings.

peace, Karen

Salads, Vegetable Side Dishes

A GREAT SALAD WITH KIDNEY BEANS AND SESAME OIL

CARROT SALAD WITH YOGURT-GINGER DRESSING

CHICKPEA SALAD WITH ROASTED PEPPERS AND SESAME-ORANGE
DRESSING

COUSCOUS SPRING SALAD

DIJON-DILL POTATO SALAD

JASMINE RICE SALAD WITH BLACK BEANS, COCONUT, AND
CORIANDER

KASHA SALAD

NOT YOUR TYPICAL THREE-BEAN SALAD

PEAR AND FETA SALAD

FRESH TOMATO-BASIL SALAD

WILTED RED CABBAGE SALAD WITH HAZELNUTS

GREEN BEANS SAUTEED WITH BASIL AND PINE NUTS

QUICK-PICKLED BEETS, JAPANESE STYLE

GINGERED BEETS COOKED WITH THEIR GREENS

HUNGARIAN STYLE BRAISED CABBAGE AND CARROTS

GLAZED CARROTS WITH RAISINS AND CASHEWS

BAKED CAULIFLOWER WITH CURRIED COCONUT-GINGER SAUCE

FENNEL AND SWEET ONIONS

KALE WITH GINGER AND GARLIC

PORTOBELLO MUSHROOM AND SPINACH SAUTÉ

SHIITAKE MUSHROOM-POTATO-LEEK MELANGE

SAUTEED MUSTARD GREENS WITH GINGER

TINY ONIONS IN CARAWAY-CREAM SAUCE

PAPRIKA POTATOES

POTATOES AND ONIONS WITH GARAM MASALA

ROASTED POTATOES

SPICY POTATOES

WHITE BEANS WITH PESTO AND TOMATO

WINTER SQUASH BAKED WITH PINE NUTS AND MAPLE SYRUP

ROASTED VEGETABLE MELANGE

Eating with the fullest pleasure...is perhaps the profoundest
enactment of our connection with the world.
   -Wendell Berry

The magic that vegetables embody has not, and I hope, will never,
cease to amaze me. A seed, tinier than a pinhead, will yield a plant taller
than me, in a matter of months. It doesn't do this alone, of course; it
needs my attention, and also water, dirt and sunlight. We're in this
together. And the outcome is a plant that nourishes not only my body,
but also my mind and spirit. I live in a world of infinite variety and end-
less possibility. It is in the fruits, vegetables, and grains of the earth that
I take this phenomena into myself and am given an opportunity to
appreciate the bounty of the earth.

For years I had a vegetable garden, a huge one- moderation is not one
of my character traits. I live in the country with nary a neighbor in view,
and the garden was a place I could usefully expend my energy and cre-
ativity while raising my two boys- in fact, I went into labor while planting onions the first time and collecting maple sap the second. My city
friends would visit, and be impressed with the garden and the babies,
then look around and see the solitude I did it in and wonder if I was
lonely. Not at all. The vegetables were my friends. They greeted me,
shiny with dew, every morning when I went out early to water and weed
before the heat galloped in. Also there to greet me were the mosquitoes
and deerflies and whatever mayhem the nightly visit of deer and wood-
chucks and rabbits left behind. Often I'd catch a groundhog in blissful
mid-munch on my brocolli, or a bunny mowing down the baby spinach.
Despite the fence and other anti-predator devices, I'd say I wasn't alone
enough. I wanted to commune with my fruits and vegetables, and not
so much with the bugs and critters who joined me in my gardening
exertions. But in gardens, as in life, we have to learn to live together or
to suffer as a consequence if we don't. Gardening was, for me, the accel-
erated course in acceptance.

My love of gardening is not different from my love of cooking.
Gardening is an inward act in which I have a silent relationship with
water, soil, sun, plants, insects, and animals. Cooking is an outward act,
in which I can nourish myself and other people, with the gift of the
plants of the earth.

A GREAT SALAD WITH KIDNEY BEANS AND SESAME OIL

One of my favorite dressings for a salad is to whisk sesame oil and lime juice together. Fresh minced coriander rounds out the flavor nicely. Here's a bean salad crunchy with lots of vegetables.

serves 4-6

6 stalks celery, sliced thinly
1 large red onion, quartered and sliced thinly
1" piece of ginger, minced
3 cloves garlic, minced
2 cups kidney beans
3 carrots, grated
1/2 cup minced parsley
1/2 cup coriander leaves, torn into pieces
1 sweet red pepper, diced
1 sweet green pepper, diced
1 cup brocolli florets, steamed
1/2 cup lime juice
1/2 cup sesame oil
salt, pepper to taste

Place all the vegetables and the beans into your serving bowl. Whisk together the lime juice and sesame oil, add to the salad, mix well, and serve.

CARROT SALAD WITH YOGURT-GINGER DRESSING

I don't know why (maybe because of its cheerful orangeyness), but carrot salad puts a smile on my face. Have fun making it, hopefully it'll make you smile, too.

serves 4

2 lbs. carrots, peeled and grated
1" piece ginger, minced
1 tbsp. fennel seeds
1/2 cup white raisins
1 small red onion, chopped fine
1 cup cauliflower florets, steamed
1 cup brocolli, steamed
1 tsp. cinnamon
1 tsp. curry powder
1 cup whole milk yogurt
salt to taste
1/2 cup walnuts, chopped (optional)
1 small head leafy green or red lettuce (not iceberg or romaine)

Place all ingredients except lettuce in a bowl and mix well. Arrange lettuce leaves on a plate or in a nice big salad bowl; mound the carrot salad artfully on top of it. You can decorate it with a sprinkle of paprika, more raisins or walnuts, or whatever your creative heart desires.

CHICKPEA SALAD WITH ROASTED PEPPERS
AND SESAME-ORANGE DRESSING

serves 4

3 large sweet peppers-red, green, and/or yellow- a combination of colors is nice
1 cup (16-oz. can) cooked chickpeas
1 medium red onion, quartered and sliced thinly
1 large tomato, cut into small dice
1 bunch cilantro leaves, minced
1/2 cup pine nuts, lightly toasted (optional)

Roast peppers by cutting them in half, removing the seeds, and placing them, skin side up, on an oiled baking dish. Put the tray under the broiler and roast the peppers. This shouldn't take more than a few minutes. You have to move the peppers around under the flame to roast them evenly. When they are soft and the skins are blackened, take them out, allow them to cool, and scrape the blackened skins off. Cut into 1" chunks.
Place all the ingredients into a bowl and mix with the dressing.

Sesame-orange dressing:

1/3 cup sesame oil
1 tbsp. each: cumin seeds, coriander powder, black mustard seeds
1 tsp. curry powder
2 tbsp. rice vinegar
1/4 cup orange juice

Place all ingredients into a jar and shake well.

COUSCOUS SPRING SALAD

serves 6-8

2 cups couscous
1/4 cup lemon juice
1/4 cup sesame oil
2 tbsp. olive oil
2 cloves garlic, minced
1 tbsp. fennel seeds
1 lb. asparagus, cut into 1" slices
1 lb. mushrooms (any kind), sliced
1 cup arugula, chopped
10 scallions, sliced thinly
fresh parsley sprigs (for garnish)

Bring 4 cups water to a boil. Add the couscous, stir, and simmer over low heat for 10 minutes, till the couscous is cooked. Mix in the lemon juice and sesame oil and allow to cool.

Meanwhile, heat olive oil in a heavy skillet. Add the garlic and fennel seeds, and sauté 10 minutes, till the garlic is browned. Stir in the asparagus and mushrooms, sauté 5-10 minutes, till the asparagus is just cooked. Turn off heat, allow to cool.

When the couscous and vegetables have cooled to room temperature, put them in a large bowl along with the arugula and scallions. Mix well, decorate with the parsley (and anything else that inspires you), and serve at room temperature or chilled.

DIJON-DILL POTATO SALAD

When making salads that call for mayonnaise, I'll often reduce the fat and calories by using half mayo and half whole milk yogurt. Potato salad works well with this variation.

serves 10-12

4 lbs. potatoes, cut into 1" dice
8 stalks celery, sliced very thin
1 large red onion, diced small
3 carrots, peeled and grated
1 cup fresh parsley, minced
1/2 cup dijon mustard
1/2 cup whole milk yogurt
1/2 cup mayonnaise
1/3 cup dill weed (fresh if possible)
salt to taste
parsley sprigs, nasturtium blossoms to garnish (optional)

Bring 3" of water to a boil in a pot large enough to hold the potatoes and put the spuds in when it does. Cover and steam 10-15 minutes, till the potatoes are done, but not mushy. Drain and rinse with cold water. Put them into a bowl with the remaining ingredients. Mix well, garnish, and serve at room temperature or chilled.

JASMINE RICE SALAD
WITH BLACK BEANS, COCONUT, AND CORIANDER

serves 8

2 cups jasmine-scented white rice
1 cup cooked black beans, rinsed and drained
juice and pulp of 1 lime
1 cup coconut milk
3 medium tomatoes, seeded and chopped
1 clove garlic, minced
1 medium red onion, diced
1 stalk lemon grass, tough outer leaves peeled off and minced
1 cup coriander leaves
1 tsp. (to taste) curry powder
1 tsp. (to taste) salt

Bring 4 cups of water to a boil, add rice, stir, bring to a boil again.
Cover and turn off the heat. The rice should be done in 10 minutes.
Place in a bowl and allow to cool. Add the the remaining ingredients,
mix well, and serve. A nice garnish could be a few coriander leaves and
a sprinkle of curry on top.

KASHA SALAD

serves 4

1 cup uncooked kasha (toasted buckwheat groats)
1 small onion, chopped finely
1 cucumber, peeled, seeded, and diced
1/2 cup minced parsley
1/2 cup chopped coriander leaves
1/4 cup sweet rice vinegar (or use cider vinegar with 1 tbsp. sugar stirred in)
1/3 cup sesame oil
1 tbsp. cumin seeds
1 tsp. salt

Bring 2 1/4 cups water to a boil in a small heavy pot. Stir in the kasha, bring to a boil again, turn off the heat, cover, and allow to fluff up. This should take about 15 minutes. Allow to cool (you can do this step earlier in the day, or a day in advance). Place the onion, cucumber, and greens into a bowl. Add the kasha, vinegar, oil, and spices, mix well, and serve.

NOT YOUR TYPICAL THREE-BEAN SALAD

What's different is the more assertive sesame oil and lime juice as the marinade.

serves 6-8

1 lb. fresh green, wax, and/or romano beans
1 large red onion, chopped
1 cup white beans (navy, cannellini, etc.), cooked
1 cup kidney beans, cooked
2 large tomatoes, chopped
1-2 jalapeno peppers, seeded and chopped (optional)
1/3 cup dark sesame oil
1/4 cup vinegar
2 tbsp. honey
2 tbsp. lime juice
1 cup coriander leaves, chopped, plus a few extra leaves for garnish
salt to taste

Prep beans and steam for 5 minutes, until just done (they should be still crispy). Drain and rinse under cold water (this keeps the green color bright). Place into a bowl and add the cooked dried beans, tomatoes and the jalapenos, if you're using them. In a small bowl, whisk together the oil, vinegar, honey, and lime juice. Stir it into the bowl of vegetables, add the chopped coriander leaves, season to taste. Garnish with the remaining coriander leaves and serve.

PEAR AND FETA SALAD

serves 6

1 quart mixed (mesclun) greens
1 red onion, quartered and sliced thinly
1 cup slivered almonds, toasted
2 bosc pears, cored, quartered, and sliced
1 cup (or more) feta cheese, crumbled
1 cup Poppyseed-Mustard Vinaigrette (see Chapter 2)

Just before serving, prepare greens and toss with onion, almonds, and pear slices. Divide between 6 salad plates. Crumble feta on salads, then drizzle dressing over them.

FRESH TOMATO-BASIL SALAD

serves 4-6

4 big, juicy, preferably garden-picked tomatoes, diced
1 cucumber, peeled and sliced
1 small red onion, quartered and sliced thinly
1 clove garlic, minced
1/4 cup olive oil
1/4 cup balsamic vinegar
6 large red leaf lettuce leaves
1/4 cup freshly grated parmesan
1/2 cup pine nuts
1/2 cup basil leaves, chopped

Place tomatoes, cucumber, and onion in a mixing bowl, mix gently. In a seperate bowl, whisk the garlic, olive oil, and vinegar. Lay lettuce leaves in a large salad bowl or small platter. Place vegetable mixture over leaves. Drizzle dressing over this, then sprinkle the parmesan, pine nuts, and basil leaves over all. Serve immediately.

WILTED RED CABBAGE SALAD WITH HAZELNUTS

serves 6-8

3 tbsp. hazelnut oil (or olive oil)
1 small onion, quartered and sliced thinly
3 cloves garlic, minced
1 medium head red cabbage, shredded
1/2 cup balsamic vinegar
1/2 cup dried currants
1/2 cup hazelnuts, chopped and toasted
1/2 lb. feta cheese, crumbled (optional)

In a large skillet, heat oil. Add onion and garlic, sauté 5-10 minutes, till browned. Add cabbage, lower heat to medium, and sauté 5 minutes, till the cabbage is wilted. Place in a bowl and toss with the balsamic vinegar, currants, and toasted hazelnuts. Sprinkle the feta over the top and serve hot or at room temperature.

GREEN BEANS SAUTEED WITH BASIL AND PINE NUTS

makes 4 servings

1 lb. green beans
2 tbsp. butter
1 clove garlic, minced
1 small onion, diced
1/2 cup pine nuts
1/2 cup fresh basil leaves, chopped
salt, pepper to taste

Prepare beans and steam them for 5 minutes. Drain. In a heavy skillet, melt butter and sauté the onion and garlic 5 minutes. Add the beans, the pine nuts, and the basil leaves, sauté 5 minutes. Season to taste and serve.

QUICK-PICKLED BEETS, JAPANESE STYLE

serves 4-6

2 tbsp. sesame oil
1 large onion, halved and sliced thinly
1/2 cup mirin (rice wine)
1 cup rice vinegar
1/2 cup vegetable stock (or water)
1/4 cup brown sugar
3 cups thinly sliced beets
1 tsp. salt

In a medium-sized heavy saucepan, heat oil. Add onion and sauté for 5 minutes. Add liquids and sugar, bring to a boil, and add the beets. Simmer over medium-low heat for 15 minutes. Salt to taste, and chill before serving. This keeps for 2 weeks, refrigerated.

GINGERED BEETS COOKED WITH THEIR GREENS

No sense in discarding the greens when you buy fresh beets. Some folks hate beets but love the greens. I'm hoping you like both in this recipe.

serves 4-6

2 lbs. beets (with their tops intact)
3 tbsp. butter or olive oil
1" piece of ginger (or more), minced
1 large white onion, chopped
2 cloves garlic, minced
1 tbsp. fennel seeds
1 tbsp. cumin seeds
1/2 cup cooking wine (or water)
1 tsp. salt

Cut tops off beets, rinse and chop coarsely. Peel beets, cut in quarters, and slice into 1/4" rounds. Heat shortening in a large heavy skillet or wok. Add onion, ginger, garlic, fennel and cumin seeds. Sauté 5 minutes. Add beets and greens, wine (or water), and salt, lower heat to medium, and simmer 15 minutes, until the beets are just cooked (they should be slightly firm). Season to taste and serve.

HUNGARIAN STYLE BRAISED CABBAGE AND CARROTS

makes 4-6 servings

2 tbsp. butter or oil
1 small red onion, sliced thinly
2 cloves garlic, minced
1 medium head cabbage, chopped
3 large carrots, sliced
1 tbsp. each: caraway seeds, dill seeds
salt, pepper to taste

Heat shortening in a large skillet. Add onion and garlic, sauté 5 minutes. Add remaining ingredients and 1 cup water, cover, and simmer till the vegetables are done, 15-20 minutes. Adjust for seasonings and serve.

GLAZED CARROTS WITH RAISINS AND CASHEWS

serves 4-6

2 tbsp. butter or oil
1 medium onion, diced small
1 lb. carrots, peeled and sliced thinly
3 tbsp. brown sugar
1/2 cup raisins
1/2 cup broken cashew pieces
1 tsp. salt
pinch pepper

Heat shortening in a large heavy skillet. Add the onion and sauté 5 minutes. Add the carrots, 1/2 cup water, and the sugar. Cover and cook over medium heat for 10 minutes. Add the raisins, cashews, and seasonings and cook 5 minutes more, stirring often. Serve hot.

BAKED CAULIFLOWER WITH CURRIED
COCONUT-GINGER SAUCE

serves 6

1 head cauliflower
1/2 recipe Curried Coconut-Ginger Sauce (see Chapter 2)
1 tbsp. curry powder

Preheat oven to 350 degrees. Trim core and leaves from cauliflower but leave the head whole. Steam 15 minutes. Carefully remove it from the steamer and rinse under cold water until cool enough to handle. In a round or square baking dish (not too much bigger than the cauliflower), spread 2 tbsp. of sauce. Pat the curry powder evenly over the cauliflower and place in the baking dish. Spoon a few more tablespoons of sauce over the cauliflower, bake 20 minutes, until light brown and slightly crispy. Place the cauliflower on a dish with the remaining sauce spooned over the top. Cut into wedges to serve.

FENNEL AND SWEET ONIONS

A little fennel goes a long way, it's a strong-tasting root. If you like fennel, though, sautéing it with lots of onions is a good way to prepare it.

serves 4-6

1/4 cup butter (or olive oil)
3 large white onions, quartered and sliced thinly
1 large fennel bulb, quartered and sliced thinly
1 tbsp. fennel seeds
salt, pepper to taste
1/2 cup fennel greens, minced

In a large, heavy skillet, heat shortening. Add onions and fennel bulb and seeds. Sauté over medium-high heat for 10-15 minutes, till the onions are deep golden brown. Season to taste, stir in the fennel greens, and serve.

KALE WITH GINGER AND GARLIC

serves 4-6

1 1/2 lbs. kale, rinsed and chopped coarsely
3 tbsp. butter or oil
1 small onion, sliced thinly
3 cloves garlic, minced
1 2" piece ginger, minced
1 tbsp. cumin seeds
1/2 tsp. salt

Steam kale for 10-15 minutes, till cooked. Pureé in a food processor or blender. In a large skillet, heat oil. Add remaining ingredients and sauté for 10-15 minutes, until onions are cooked and golden brown. Add puréed kale, mix well, and cook for 5 minutes, till heated through. Serve hot.

PORTOBELLO MUSHROOM AND SPINACH SAUTÉ

serves 4-6

1 1/2 lbs. fresh spinach
1/4 cup extra virgin olive oil
3 cloves garlic (or more), minced
1 medium red onion, quartered and sliced thinly
4 large portobello mushrooms, sliced 1/4" thick
1/2 tsp. salt
1/4 cup each: minced fresh oregano, thyme, and coriander
(or substitute 1 tbsp. each of dried herbs)
pepper to taste

Rinse the spinach and chop spinach coarsely (leave the stems on,
unless they're stringy or tough). In a large skillet or wok, heat oil. Add
garlic and onion, sauté over medium heat for 5 minutes. Add
mushrooms and sprinkle with salt, sauté a few minutes till they start to
sweat. Lower heat, cover, and cook for 5 minutes, till almost soft. Add
the spinach, raise heat to medium, cover. Cook for 5-10 minutes,
stirring often, till the spinach is cooked through. Add the herbs and
season to taste. If the dish is too watery, cook, uncovered, over high
heat for a minute or two to evaporate the water.

SHIITAKE MUSHROOM-POTATO-LEEK MELANGE

serves 4-6

3 tbsp. olive oil
1 large onion, chopped
2 cloves garlic
3 large potatoes, cut into 1" dice
3 leeks, trimmed, rinsed, and cut into 1" slices
1 lb. fresh shiitake mushrooms, sliced
1 tbsp. rosemary leaves
salt, pepper

Heat oil in a heavy pot. Add onions and garlic, sauté 5 minutes. Add potatoes, mushrooms, and leeks, sauté 5 minutes, then pour in 1 cup water. Lower heat to medium-low, cover, and simmer 20 minutes, until the potatoes are cooked. Stir occasionally, and add water if needed. Toss on rosemary leaves, season to taste, and serve over rice.

SAUTEÉD MUSTARD GREENS WITH GINGER

serves 4-6

2 tbsp. sesame oil
1 medium onion, diced
2" piece ginger, minced
2 cloves garlic
1 1/2 lbs. mustard greens, chopped
1/4 cup rice vinegar
1 tbsp. brown sugar
1/2 tsp. salt

Heat oil in a large frying pan. Add onion, ginger, and garlic, sauté until golden, about 10 minutes. Add greens and sauté over medium heat for 5 minutes. Whisk the vinegar, sugar, and salt until the sugar is dissolved, then add it to the greens. Stir, cover, and cook over medium-low heat until the greens are done, about 10 minutes.

TINY ONIONS IN CARAWAY-CREAM SAUCE

serves 4

simmered onions:
3 tbsp. olive oil or butter
1 pint baby onions, peeled
2 cloves garlic, minced
1/2 cup vegetable stock (or water)
1 tbsp. caraway seeds

cream sauce:
2 tbsp. olive oil or butter
3 tbsp. flour
2 cups milk or cream
salt, pepper to taste

To prepare the onions, heat oil or butter in a large skillet. Add onions and garlic, sauté 5 minutes. Add the stock (or water) and caraway seeds, cover, and simmer 20 minutes, till the onions are soft.

Meanwhile, make the cream sauce: In a small heavy saucepan, make a roux by heating the shortening and whisking in the flour rapidly till it gets a toasty look and smell. This should take only two or three minutes. Next, carefully stir in the milk or cream slowly, whisking all the while. Lower the heat and allow the sauce to thicken, about 3-5 minutes. When the sauce is done, stir it into the onions, check for seasonings, and serve.

PAPRIKA POTATOES

The marriage of paprika- lots of it- to potatoes is a happy one. If you can get real Hungarian paprika at a gourmet shop, so much the better. In Hungary paprika is a cash crop and also a cultural event. Varieties of paprika abound- it is in the same botanical family as green peppers- and ranges from mild, which is the paprika we know of in this country, to very hot.

serves 4

3 tbsp. butter or oil
3 cloves garlic, minced
1 small onion, chopped
4-5 large white potatoes, cut into 2" dice
3 stalks celery, sliced thinly
1/4 cup paprika powder
1 tsp. salt
1 tsp. pepper
4 scallions, cut into very thin slices

Heat oil or butter in a medium saucepan. Add garlic and onion and sauté 5 minutes. Add 1 cup water and the paprika, mix well, and add the potatoes and celery. Lower heat to medium-low, cover, and simmer until the potatoes are done, about 20 minutes. Check for seasonings, stir in the scallions, and serve.

The Hungarian way to serve this would be with a little sour cream on the side, to stir in. Or use whole milk yogurt. Or neither- these potatoes are fine the way they are, and get better if allowed to hang out in your refrigerator for a day or two before serving.

POTATOES AND ONIONS WITH GARAM MASALA

makes 8 servings

6 large white potatoes, cut in 1/2" slices
1 large sweet potato, cut in 1/2" slices
1 medium red onion, quartered and sliced thinly
1 large carrot, grated
1 cup milk or half-and-half
1 egg
1 tbsp. garam masala (A special spice mixture you'll find at
Indian markets. A reasonable substitute is to mix equal parts
curry, cinnamon, and cardamon powder)
1 tsp. salt
3 tbsp. butter

Preheat oven to 375 degrees. Places potatoes, onion, and carrot in a
greased casserole dish, preferably one with a cover. In a small bowl,
beat the milk or half-and-half, egg, and spices, pour over the vegetables.
Cut butter into tiny pieces and dot the top of the casserole, cover with
foil, and bake for 45 minutes.

ROASTED POTATOES

When you've already got a casserole in the oven, roasted potatoes are an easy, speedy side dish to throw in alongside. This is one of those pleases-everybody recipes that is quick to put together and quick to disappear.

serves 6-8

5 lbs. potatoes, preferably new potatoes; a combination of red, white, and Yukon Gold is nice
1/2 cup olive oil
1 tbsp. salt
1/4 cup dried rosemary leaves
freshly ground black pepper (optional)

This is a great way to prepare those tiny newly-picked potatoes called "baby potatoes". If you are using them, rinse them and place them in a 9"x13" casserole dish. If you are using larger potatoes cut them into 1" dice, and put them in your casserole dish. Rub the potatoes so that they are evenly coated with oil, then evenly rub the rosemary and salt on. Grind black pepper over all, and put the dish in a preheated 400 degree oven for 45 minutes (if you are putting this in with something else that requires a 350 degree oven, bake them for an hour, maybe more. The potatoes should be brown and crispy outside and soft inside). Serve hot.

Should you have leftovers, these potatoes make yummy potato salad and are great in omelets.

SPICY POTATOES

serves 6

3 tbsp. shortening
2 clove garlic, minced
2" piece ginger, peeled and minced
1 large onion, quartered and diced
1 tbsp. each: cumin, coriander, and black mustard seeds
6 potatoes, diced into 1" cubes
1 cup fresh (or frozen) peas
1 tsp. curry powder
salt to taste

Heat shortening in a heavy pot. Add garlic, ginger, onion, and seeds, sauté 5 minutes. Add potatoes and 1 cup water, simmer over low heat until potatoes are cooked, about 20 minutes. Add peas and seasonings, cook 5 minutes more, and serve. Or use to stuff into samosas or wrap in phyllo dough.

WHITE BEANS WITH PESTO AND TOMATO

serves 6-8

3 tbsp. olive oil
4 cloves garlic, minced
1 large onion, diced
3 cups white (navy) beans, cooked
1/2 cup Basil Pesto (see Chapter 2)
1 large tomato, chopped
1/2 cup minced parsley
1 tsp. (to taste) salt

Heat oil in a large skillet. Add garlic and onion, sauté till golden brown, about 10 minutes. Add beans and pesto, lower heat, and cook 10 minutes more. Stir in the tomato, sprinkle the parsley over, and serve.

WINTER SQUASH BAKED
WITH PINE NUTS AND MAPLE SYRUP

serves 4-6

1 butternut squash
4 tbsp. butter
1/4 cup maple syrup
1 tsp. ground coriander
1 tsp.salt
1 tsp. ground cardamon
1/2 cup pine nuts, toasted

Preheat oven to 350 degrees. Peel squash, cut in half, and scoop out seeds. Cut into 1" dice. Place into a small casserole dish, dot with butter. Drizzle the maple syrup over the squash, sprinkle with the salt and spices. Bake, covered with foil, for 30 minutes. Spread the pine nuts over the top and serve.

ROASTED VEGETABLE MELANGE

makes 6-8 servings

This dish, like Roasted Potatoes, is great to put in the oven when something else is already in there. And it's a fine alternative to the usual steamed or sautéed preparation we usually do with vegetables.

serves 6-8

2 large onions, cut in half and then each half quartered
6 cloves (or more) garlic
2 quarts vegetables, cut into 1" dice- can include
carrots, green peppers, brocolli,potatoes, yams,
cauliflower, winter squash (soft or leafy things,
like tomatoes and spinach, do not work in this recipe)
3/4 cup olive oil
1 tbsp salt
1 tbsp. each: dried thyme, oregano, rosemary, dill

Place onions, garlic, and vegetables in a 9"x13" casserole dish. Rub evenly with oil, then add the herbs and salt; evenly mix them in. Bake in a 350 degree oven for 45 minutes-1 hour. Baking time is determined by the types of vegetables you use- the more root vegetables you have, the longer time it takes to bake. Peppers take the least amount of time. Check the oven after about 20 minutes of baking, and stir the veggies around a bit.

These vegetables are best served piping hot out of the oven. Whatever's left over can be stuffed in a pita with a little hummos and sprouts for tomorrow's lunch.

Chutnies, Sauces, Pesto

BANANA CHUTNEY

TOMATO-TAMARIND CHUTNEY

BUTTERMILK-HORSERADISH SAUCE

CURRIED COCONUT-GINGER-PEANUT SAUCE

PEANUT-GINGER SAUCE

BASIL PESTO

CORIANDER PESTO

SUNDRIED TOMATO PESTO

LEMON-DILL BECHAMEL (AS CREPE FILLING)

ORIENTAL MARINADE

POPPYSEED-MUSTARD VINAIGRETTE

There is nothing to eat,
seek it where you will,
but the body of the Lord.

The blessed plants
and the sea, yield it
to the imagination

intact.

-William Carlos Williams

This chapter covers the enhancements- the chutnies and sauces that provide the flourishes that enhance a meal. Dab a bit of chutney next to whatever has become standard fare in your kitchen and experience the "big aha!" Or build a meal from the inspiration that a sauce provides. Do you want it to be the finishing touch to your crepes? Or to just make a simple pot of rice or couscous, with the sauce being the essence of what binds and completes your fare? One of the great things about sauces and pestos is that they can be made ahead of time. When you're out of time or energy to cook, just cook up some grains or pasta, mix it with pesto, and call it dinner.

The word pesto is derived from the same Latin root as pestle (as in "mortar and..."). In the Dark Ages, before the invention of the Cuisinart, pestos were made with that humble kitchen implement. I have mortar-and-pestled all three of the pestos featured here, just to say that I have done it. It's a lot of work, but if you have the time, a shady spot in your yard on a hot summer day, a breeze floating by, and a frosty glass of lemonade, it is so worth it. The added benefit is a good upper-body workout. The taste of the pesto is the same as if you use a food processor, but the texture is courser and there is a subtlety that is lost if you use a machine. You also miss out on the aroma that grinding by hand will give you. Grinding basil and coriander by hand releases the essence of the herbs into the air. And so your small act of smashing nuts and herbs becomes a larger event, as the molecules of scent are released into the world. It is in the little gestures of cooking that I have seen that we are connected, and so, everything I do matters.

And usually, what matters is that I get the meal out in time. So I use the Cuisinart.

BANANA CHUTNEY

This is good alongside a spicy Thai or Indian meal. Or make a simple
pot of rice and steam some vegetables and tofu. Banana chutney on the
plate will keep you from getting bored with this healthy but otherwise
blasé meal.

makes about 3 cups

4 very ripe bananas
2" piece of ginger, peeled and cut into small pieces
1/4 cup lime juice
1/2 cup grated unsweetened coconut
1 tsp. salt
1/2 tsp. clove powder
1/4 cup coriander leaves

Place all ingredients in a food processor, pureé till smooth.
This does not keep well; it should be eaten the day it is made.

TOMATO-TAMARIND CHUTNEY

Tamarinds are the long seedpods that dangle from the tamarind tree in Asia. It's shape looks like a giant green bean (only it's brown); the sour, fleshy pulp surrounding the hard beans inside is what's used to make tamarind paste.

makes 4 cups (about)

1/4 cup butter
2 large onions, chopped
6 cloves garlic, minced
5 (or more) chilis (your choice), minced
2 tbsp. cumin seeds
1/2 cup tamarind concentrate
1/2 cup brown sugar
2 lbs. plum tomatoes, chopped
1 tbsp. salt

In heavy saucepan, heat butter. Add onions and garlic and sauté over medium-high heat until they are deep brown, about 20 minutes. Add the remaining ingredients and simmer, stirring, over medium heat for 20 minutes, or until the chutney is fairly thick and spreadable. Chill before serving; this keeps well in the refrigerator for 2 weeks, and you can freeze it.

This is great to serve with samosas, pakoras, and other Indian delights, but you needn't limit yourself to that; this is also a great dip, sandwich spread, or a nice meal accompaniment to leftovers.

BUTTERMILK-HORSERADISH SAUCE

This is good served over stuffed peppers or tossed with pasta.

makes 2 cups

2 tbsp. butter
3 tbsp. flour
1 cup buttermilk
1 egg
3 tbsp. milk or cream
1/4 cup horseradish
1/2 cup grated sharp cheddar

In a heavy saucepan, make a roux: melt the butter and whisk in the flour. Cook over medium heat, whisking constantly, until the flour becomes toasted brown. Slowly pour in the buttermilk, whisking all the while, and simmer 5 minutes, until the sauce is thickened. In a small bowl, beat the egg with the milk or cream and slowly pour this into the saucepan, whisking constantly so that the egg doesn't cook. After a minute of whisking, stir in the horseradish and cheese, cook over medium-low heat for 5 minutes, stirring. When the cheese is melted, the sauce is done.

This sauce freezes well, and keeps in the refrigerator for up to a week.

CURRIED COCONUT-GINGER-PEANUT SAUCE

There's something about the combination of peanuts, coconut, curry, and ginger, that people love. I know people who have dedicated their lives to disliking anything that is not straight-ahead bland American fare. When I can get them to try this sauce, they are moved to reconsider their position.

makes almost 2 cups

1 cup peanut butter
1 2" piece ginger, peeled and cut into small chunks
3 cloves garlic
1 tbsp. curry powder
1 tsp cumin seeds
1 tbsp. coriander seeds
3/4 cup coconut milk
1 tsp. salt

Place all ingredients in a food processor and pureé till smooth. This keeps, refrigerated, for 2 weeks.

PEANUT-GINGER SAUCE

makes approximately 2 cups

3" piece ginger, peeled and cut into chunks
1/2 cup shelled peanuts
1 cup unsweetened peanut butter
1/4 cup rice vinegar

Place ginger and peanuts into a food processor or blender. Chop finely, add the peanut butter and vinegar, mix well. This sauce keeps,
refrigerated, for up to a month.

BASIL PESTO

The aroma of fresh basil brings the hot, sultry days of August into my kitchen any time of year. I grow basil and make lots and lots of pesto to freeze. You can visit a farmer's market to obtain large quantities. Or try growing it yourself - its requirements are space, sun, and water.

makes 2+ cups

1 quart basil leaves
3-6 cloves garlic, peeled
1/2 cup parmesan cheese
1/2 cup (or more) olive oil
1/2 cup pine nuts (in a pinch, you can substitute walnut pieces)
1/2 tsp. salt

Place all ingredients in the workbowl of your food processor and whir till smooth. You may need to add a little more olive oil if the pesto is too thick.

Pesto keeps in the refrigerator for weeks. Pour a little bit of olive oil over the top to keep it from blackening, which it will do. The blackened part of the pesto is fine to use, and underneath, all the pesto will be bright green and lovely.

CORIANDER PESTO

One year I gave in to my love of coriander and grew what seemed to be acres of it. Well, it all matured at the same time, and if you don't harvest it right away, it will bolt and go to seed, and the leaves will get rangy and thin. So there I was, with wheelbarrows full of coriander leaves and not enough neighbors to give it away to. Coriander pesto was born. It freezes well.

makes 1 1/2 cups (about)

4 cloves garlic
1/2 cup roasted cashews
1/4 cup sesame oil
1/2 cup parmesan cheese
3-4 cups fresh coriander leaves
1 tsp. salt

Place garlic and cashews into a food processor, chop finely. Add the remaining ingredients and pureé until smooth (you may need to add a little more oil). This keeps well in the refrigerator for a week.

SUNDRIED TOMATO PESTO

makes about 1 1/2 cups

6 cloves garlic
1 cup sundried tomatoes
1/2 cup walnuts
1/2 cup olive oil
1 tsp. salt

In a food processor, mince the garlic. Add the remaining ingredients and chop finely. This will probably not get really smooth, but it is better when it's a little chunky. This keeps in the refrigerator for 2 weeks, and it freezes well.

LEMON-DILL BECHAMEL (AS CREPE FILLING)

Bechamel sauce is a decadence of French descent. Here I suggest it as a filling for crepes. Other ideas are to pour a little, just a little, over steamed asparagus or other vegetables, or to toss it with egg noodles.

makes about 2 cups

1/2 c. butter
2 cloves garlic, minced
1 small onion, inced
3 tbsp. flour
1 egg, lightly beaten
1 cup milk or cream
1 cup parmesan cheese
1/4 c. dill weed
3 tbsp. lemon juice
1 tsp. grated lemon peel
1 tsp. salt

In a small skillet, heat 1/4 cup of the butter and sauté the garlic and onions until they are golden brown, about 10 minutes. Make a roux: in a small saucepan, melt remaining butter and stir in the flour, whisking until it smells toasty. Mix the egg and milk together and slowly pour it into the roux, whisking quickly. After a few minutes, it should thicken and you can add the cheese, dill weed, lemon juice and peel, and salt. Stir while the mixture blends and thickens, about 5 minutes. You can refrigerate or freeze this if you are not using it right away.

To make crepes, spread about 1/2 cup of the bechamel in a stripe across the middle of a crepe. Roll it up, place on your serving tray. If you are serving these right away, keep the serving tray in a warm (not hot) oven, till they are all done, then serve. If you are serving these later (you can prep up to a day ahead), warm in a 300-degree oven for 20-30 minutes.

ORIENTAL MARINADE

A versatile marinade, good for grilled vegetables, tofu, or tempeh.

makes 2 -3 cups

1/2 cup rice vinegar
1/2 cup sesame oil
1/2 cup mirin (or cooking wine)
1 cup water
1/4 cup tamari
1 tbsp. cumin seeds
1 tbsp. coriander seeds
3 cloves, minced
1 tbsp. dried oregano
3 dried shiitake (or other) mushrooms

Place all ingredients into a pot, bring to a boil, and simmer 15 minutes. Take out the mushrooms, mince them, and return them to the pot. Simmer 5 minutes more, then pour it over whatever you intend to grill, or store it, refrigerated, for up to 1 month.

POPPYSEED-MUSTARD VINAIGRETTE

makes 2 cups

1/4 cup poppyseeds
1/2 cup dijon mustard
3/4 cup olive oil
3/4 cup cider vinegar
1 tsp. salt
1/2 tsp. pepper

Place all ingredients into a jar and shake well. This keeps, refrigerated, for up to 2 weeks.

Dips, Sandwich Fillings, Appetizers

DELICIOUS SPINACH DIP

HORSERADISH DIP

HUMMOS

HUNGARIAN PAPRIKA CREAM CHEESE DIP

SESAME EGGPLANT DIP

TAHINI-AVOCADO DIP

AVOCADO-TAHINI-GINGER COMBO

SUNNY TOFU SALAD

T.V.P. SLOPPY JOES WITH SHIITAKE MUSHROOMS

COCONUT-POTATO SAMOSAS

SPINACH AND CHEESE BALLS

STUFFED OLIVES, GREEK-STYLE

Poets make the best cooks. Prose writers, the most appreciative friends of poets.

-Joyce Carol Oates

I have a confession to make. I am not a big fan of hors d'oeuvres. I don't know why, exactly, but I think it has something to do with those weddings and bar mitzvahs I was subjected to attend when I was a kid. Those things seemed to drag on for days, not hours, and there was nothing to do but eat. I was awkward and shy and found solace and entertainment in the awful puffs and skewered things being passed around. To this day, when I think of hors d'oeuvres, I have an unfortunate mental association of them with boredom and mild nausea.

But I'm a caterer! People want hors d'oeuvres! And I make them, cheerfully, but I haven't gotten creative about them, so I follow other people's recipes (more or less). Crudite platters are great fun for me, though, they're like sculptures using my favorite art supplies-vegetables.

There are a few recipes for appetizers in this chapter, for the kind you can make in advance and serve up easily when your guests arrive. That way you can hang out with your guests and not have to spend your time at your own party in the kitchen (though that's where most parties end up, anyway). The dips and patés in this chapter are also good if made in advance- in fact, they're better that way. And you can make sandwiches the next day from any dip that's left over- spread a little on bread or a pita or tortilla, add sprouts and tomato slices, and you've got lunch.

DELICIOUS SPINACH DIP

makes 3+ cups

3 tbsp. olive oil
1 large onion, chopped
4 cloves garlic, minced
1 lb. mushrooms, sliced thinly
2 lbs. spinach (fresh or frozen), cooked and drained thoroughly
1 12-oz. jar roasted red peppers, drained
3 cups sour cream
1 tsp. fennel seeds
1 tsp. each: dried oregano, thyme, and tarragon
salt, pepper to taste

Heat oil in a large skillet. Add onion and garlic, sauté 10 minutes. Add mushrooms, sauté 10-15 minutes more, till they are cooked and the liquid is steamed off. Place the cooked spinach and the roasted peppers into a food processor and pureé. Place this in a large bowl with the sauteédvegetables and the remaining ingredients, mix well. Chill and serve.

You can make this up to 2 days in advance; the flavor improves on standing.

HORSERADISH DIP

makes about 1 1/2 cups

1/2 cup prepared horseradish, liquid drained out as much as possible
8 oz. cream cheese, softened
1/4 cup plain whole milk yogurt
2 tbsp. mustard (preferably brown)
1 tbsp. honey

Place all ingredients in a food processor till smooth.
You can serve this as a dip, or put it in a pastry bag and use it as a topping for crackers, cucumber slices, and/or hardboiled egg halves.

HUMMOS

This is the classic hummos preparation. Feel free to be creative; add more garlic, more lemon juice. Put in roasted vegetables, even a chili pepper or two.

makes 2-3 cups

2-4 cloves garlic
2 cups well-cooked chickpeas
1/2 cup tahini
1/2 cup lemon juice (fresh-squeezed is best)
1 tsp. (to taste) salt
1 tbsp. cumin seeds (optional)

Place garlic cloves in a food processor; mince. Add the remaining ingredients, pureé till smooth. Add a little water if you like it thinner. This keeps in the refrigerator for a week and freezes well.

HUNGARIAN PAPRIKA CREAM CHEESE DIP

Another dish of my youth, my mom made this whenever company came over. At least one person would always ask for the recipe.

makes 2-3 cups

8 oz. cream cheese, softened
1 cup sour cream (or whole milk yogurt)
1 tbsp. garlic powder
1/4 cup good-quality paprika
2 tsp. salt
2 tsp. caraway seeds
3 tbsp. worcestershire sauce (omit if you avoid all animal products- this has anchovies in it)
6 scallions, sliced thinly

Place all ingredients, except scallions, in a blender or food processor, and pureé. Place in a bowl and stir in all but 3 tablespoons scallions in, mix well. When serving, sprinkle the rest of the scallions and a pinch more paprika over the top. This is good with crudites, or spread on rye toast with a pimento or black olive slice for decoration.

SESAME EGGPLANT DIP

makes about 1 quart

2 large eggplants
2 cups plain whole milk yogurt
1/4 cup sesame oil
2 tsp. salt
1 tbsp. (or more) each: cumin seeds, coriander seeds, garlic powder,
chili powder
1/2 cup fresh parsley, minced

Roast eggplants by slicing the tops off and placing them on a greased
baking dish for 20 minutes at 400 degrees. Drain and peel. Place into
food processor with the remaining ingredients, pureé. Serve at room
temperature with chips, pita bread, and/or crudites.

TAHINI-AVOCADO DIP

makes about 3 cups dip

3 large very ripe avocados
1 medium onion
3/4 cup tahini
1 medium tomato
1 tsp. curry powder
1 tsp. cumin seeds
1 tsp. salt
the juice of 1 lemon (1/3 cup)
1/2 cup fresh coriander leaves
paprika

Place all ingredients in a food processor and pureé till smooth.
Pour into serving bowl and sprinkle with paprika.

AVOCADO-TAHINI-GINGER COMBO

makes about 3 cups

2" piece of ginger, peeled
2 cloves garlic, peeled
2 very ripe avocadoes
1/4 cup lime juice
1/2 cup tahini
8 oz. soft tofu
2 tsp. salt
curry powder, to taste
cayenne (optional)

Mince the ginger and garlic in your food processor. Add the remaining ingredients and pureé till smooth. Check for seasonings, and serve. This keeps in the refrigerator for a week; it's great "fast food" to have around. You can make a quick meal by stuffing pita bread with this, or stirring it into rice or noodles, with a chopped tomato or two.

SUNNY TOFU SALAD

This is a great pita-bread stuffer, along with sliced tomato and sprouts.

serves 4

1 lb firm tofu, drained
4 carrots, grated
1 cup shredded red cabbage
1 small onion, chopped
2 tbsp. mayonnaise
1/4 cup whole milk yogurt
1 tbsp. garam masala
1 tsp. coriander powder
1/2 tsp. salt

Squeeze all the water you can out of the tofu. Mash it well, then add the other ingredients. (Using your hands to mix this is the easiest and most thorough way). Chill before serving.

T.V.P. SLOPPY JOES WITH SHIITAKE MUSHROOMS

Those of us who came of age in the 60's and 70's and leaned towards the natural-foods lifestyle know what t.v.p., or textured vegetable protein, is. Back then it was a trendy food that was touted to be a great substitute for ground beef, as it has a grainy, somewhat chewy texture, and is protein-rich. You can find it in health food stores, and it's a good ingredient for stews and for these vegetarian sloppy joes.

serves 6

3 tbsp. canola oil
1 large onion, diced small
2 cloves garlic, minced
1 lb. shiitake mushrooms, sliced thinly
1 1/2 cups water
1 cup t.v.p.
1 cup barbeque sauce
6 kaiser rolls (or hamburger buns)

Heat oil in a medium-sized heavy pot. Add onions and garlic and sauté for 5 minutes. Stir in the shiitake mushrooms and sauté 5 minutes more. Add water, bring to a boil, then pour in t.v.p. Bring to a boil again, cover, and turn off heat. In 10 minutes the t.v.p. should be expanded and ready to eat. Add the barbeque sauce, stir well.

Cut the rolls in half, place, open-faced, on a platter. Spoon the t.v.p. mixture over the bottom half of each roll, put the top on, and serve.

COCONUT-POTATO SAMOSAS

Always on the menu at Indian restaurants in the appetizer section of the menu, samosas are good as the focus of a meal, as well. Serve with a bit of basmati rice, chutney, and a bowl of soup.

makes 12-15 samosas (depending on how big you make them)

dough:
1 stick (1/2 cup) butter or margarine
1 cup unbleached white flour
1/2 cup whole wheat flour
1/2 cup ice water

filling:
2 tbsp. butter
3 tbsp. minced ginger
3 garlic cloves, minced
chili peppers, to taste, minced (optional)
1 tbsp. cumin seeds
1 tbsp. coriander seeds
3 large white potatoes, cut into 1" dice
1 cup coconut milk
1/2 cup chopped peanuts
2 tsp. salt
1 egg, beaten

Make the dough: Cut the butter into chunks and place in your food processor along with the flours. Turn the processor on and slowly pour the water in (not all of it) until the dough forms a firm ball that doesn't stick to the workbowl. You may need to add more flour. Take out the dough, wrap, and refrigerate for at least one hour.

Make the filling: Heat the butter in a heavy pot. Add the ginger, onion, garlic, and cumin seeds, sauté 10 minutes. Add the remaining ingredients and simmer, uncovered, until the potatoes are just cooked (stir frequently).

Make the samosas: Preheat oven to 350 degrees. Grease 2-3 cookie sheets. Take out the dough, divide into 12-15 pieces. Roll one piece into a ball, flatten it, and place it in front of you. Roll it out to a circle with a rolling pin. Place a little filling in the circle, fold over so the edges meet, and press the edges together. You may want to seal the edges by brushing them, before you fold them over, with a little beaten egg. Place the samosa on your cookie sheet and repeat the process till all the samosas are done. Brush with the remaining egg and bake for 25 minutes, till they are golden brown. Serve hot, with a variety of chutneys as an accompaniment, if you wish.

SPINACH AND CHEESE BALLS

makes about 75 (small) appetizers

2 cups cooked spinach (can be fresh or frozen), drained well
1 1/2 cups corn chips
1 cup bread crumbs
1 cup mixed fresh herbs- basil, arugula, dill
1/2 cup (1 stick) butter or margarine
2 eggs
1 1/2 cups grated parmesan cheese

Put spinach, corn chips, bread crumbs, and herbs into a food processor, blend till all ingredients are chopped finely. Add shortening, eggs, and cheese, pureé till smooth. Preheat oven to 350 degrees. Grease 2-3 cookie sheets. Roll the dough into balls about 1 1/2" in diameter, place on cookie sheets (they can be placed close together-they won't expand). Bake for 15 minutes, till they are golden brown. (You can bake these halfway through and then refrigerate or freeze them until you are ready to serve them). Serve hot, stuck with toothpicks, alongside a nice salsa accompaniment.

STUFFED OLIVES, GREEK-STYLE

makes 30 olives

2 cups cooked white rice
1/2 cup extra virgin olive oil
1/2 cup mint leaves, minced
3 tbsp. dill weed
1/2 cup feta cheese, crumbled into tiny bits
1/2 tsp. salt (to taste)
30 colossal olives (2 16-oz. cans, about)

Mix the first 6 ingredients well, stuff them into the olives, and serve. Easy. No problem. Yum.

Breads, Crepes, Quiches, Stuffings

BASIC WHOLE WHEAT-HONEY BREAD

BREAD STUFFED WITH SUNDRIED TOMATO PESTO AND KALAMATA

OLIVES

CARROT BREAD WITH CARDAMOM AND GINGER

OATMEAL-WALNUT BREAD

FRESH CORN CORNBREAD

JALAPENO CHEESE CORN BREAD

CORNBREAD-CHEESE PUDDING WITH FRESH HERBS

BASIC CREPES

CORN, BASIL, AND CHEESE FILLING FOR CREPES

CARROT-SCALLION QUICHE WITH BUTTERMILK

EGGPLANT QUICHE

ONION PIE

TOFU PIE WITH HERBS AND BLACK OLIVES- NO DAIRY

CHESTNUT STUFFING, FOR SQUASH OR TURKEY

The poet and the baker are brothers in the essential task of nourishing the world.

        -Isabelle Allende

Everybody loves bread, especially a loaf made by familiar hands, a loaf freshly pulled from the oven, hot and aromatic. The birth of bread requires a gestation period lasting 4 to 24 hours (or longer, if you are making sourdough). And, like every birth, vigorous effort is required to begin the process. You have to put the ingredients together, mix well, then knead them for at least a quarter of an hour. The rest is mindful waiting; the magic happens outside of any effort of your own. Give your loaves warmth, darkness, and time, and they will do the rest.

I love the physical nature of bread-making; to me, using a bread machine would defeat the purpose. To have bread ready for lunch, I start at breakfast. The ingredients are on the table. The bowls and towels are nearby. There's good music plugged into the CD player, something I can dance to. When my arms are working the dough the rest of me just doesn't stand there; my feet, my legs like to get in on the act of bringing forth another loaf of bread into the world to feed people and make them happy.

So, have fun with it. The only way to learn how to bake bread is by baking bread. Read all the recipes you want, but you'll only know the process by getting your hands and your heart into the flour, water, and yeast. Some people get it right away, some people bake bricks. I was one of the latter, and I still bake bricks sometimes. They make great breadcrumbs. Or stuffing. Or I just serve them anyway; they're hot, they smell great, they're just a little dense (aren't we all, sometimes?). Slice it thin, smile as you present your loaf that all your love has gone into, and people will love it. And you.

BASIC WHOLE WHEAT-HONEY BREAD

This is it, the bread I've made hundreds of times. Don't forget to smile and knead some joy into your loaves. It makes a difference.

makes 5 1 1/2 lb. loaves

6-8 cups whole wheat flour
6-8 cups unbleached white flour
3 tbsp. yeast
5 tsp. salt
1/2 cup honey
1/2 cup canola oil
1/2 cup sunflower seeds
1 small egg, beaten

Place 6 cups of each kind of flour in a large bowl. Add the yeast, salt, and honey. Have 1 quart warm water handy. Pour half the water into the bowl, mix with your hands. Start mixing this well, adding flour, then water, until you have a good, solid, pliable ball of dough that no longer sticks to your hands. Spread some more flour (about 1 cup) on your kneading surface, then turn the dough out onto this. Start kneading.

As you get more experience with bread-making, you will know what the consistency of your dough should be, and when to stop kneading. If this is your debut as a bread-maker, trust your instincts, and above all, have fun. Bread is very forgiving.

When you're done kneading the dough (15 minutes is about right), put it into a large bowl, rub oil all over it, cover the bowl with a towel. Let the dough rise for 1 1/2 hours in a warm (100 degrees) place. When the dough has doubled in size, punch it down and allow it to rise again, in a warm place, for 1 hour.

Grease 5 loaf pans. Punch the dough down again, and divide into 5 pieces. Knead each piece, shape it into a smooth ball, and place it into a pan. It should take up 1/3 of the pan. Brush the breads with the beaten egg, sprinkle with sunflower seeds, and allow to rise for 45 minutes. Put them in a preheated 350 degree oven for 1/2 hour. They are done when they sound hollow when rapped on the bottom. Take out of the pans immediately to cool.

BREAD STUFFED WITH SUNDRIED TOMATO PESTO AND KALAMATA OLIVES

Once you've mastered the basic whole wheat-honey loaf, you can embellish by stuffing the loaves. The basic dough makes 5-6 loaves, so this recipe will make about the same (although I always end up using more dough when I stuff the loaves). Figure on ending up with 4, maybe 5 loaves.

for each loaf you are making, you need:

1/2 cup chopped kalamata olives
1/2 cup sundried tomato pesto (see Chapter 2)
1/2 cup grated mozzarella cheese
1 small egg, beaten
poppyseeds

The dough should be on its third rise, ready for baking. Press it out and flatten it as best you can, making it into a rectangle. In the center, spread the pesto, olives, and cheese. Fold the dough over on each end, sealing in the filling, then roll it, jellyroll style. Place it into a greased loaf pan. Brush with beaten egg, sprinkle with poppyseeds, and allow to rise 45 minutes in a warm (100 degree) place. Bake for 30 minutes, turn out onto a cutting board, and serve.

CARROT BREAD WITH CARDAMOM AND GINGER

Though sweet enough to be a dessert, this bread is also a good side dish to a spicy stew or soup. Try it with Mulligatawny (Chapter 5) or Caribbean-style Vegetable Stew with Peanut Sauce (Chapter 6).

makes 1 loaf

1/4 cup honey
1/4 cup butter or oil
2 eggs
1 cup whole wheat flour
1 1/2 cups unbleached white flour
1 tsp. baking powder
1 tsp. baking soda
2 carrots, grated
2 tsp. cardamom powder
1" cube ginger, grated

Preheat oven to 350 degrees. Mix together honey, oil, and eggs. In a seperate bowl, mix the flours and baking powder and soda. Beat the contents of the dry ingredients into the wet. Stir in the carrots, cardamom, and ginger. Pour into a greased loaf pan and bake for 45 minutes-1 hour, when a tester comes out clean and the loaf is golden brown.

OATMEAL-WALNUT BREAD

makes 3-4 loaves

2 pkg. (2 tbsp.) baking yeast
2 tbsp. honey
4 cups whole wheat bread flour
5 (or more) cups unbleached white flour
2 cups cooked oatmeal
3 tbsp. salt
3 tbsp. canola oil
1 cup broken walnut pieces
1 small egg, beaten
rolled oats, sunflower seeds, or poppyseeds, for topping the loaves
(optional)

Dissolve yeast in 3 cups warm water, stir in honey. Add flours, salt, oil and 2 more cups water. Begin to knead, adding the oatmeal about 1/2 cup at a time. You may need to add water, or flour, to get it to the right elasticity for kneading. Work the dough for 5 minutes, then add the walnut pieces and knead 5-10 minutes more. Put it in a large bowl, rub the dough with oil, cover it with a towel, and place in a warm (100 degrees) place, such as a preheated oven, for one hour.

After an hour, the dough should be doubled in size. Punch it down, knead it briefly, rub it with oil, and allow it to rise again. After 45 minutes, take out the dough, punch it down, and divide into 3-4 equal pieces. Knead each piece briefly, then place each ball of dough into a loaf pan. The dough should take up 1/3 of the pan. Brush each loaf generously with the beaten egg, sprinkle with the oatmeal and/or seeds, then allow to rise in a warm place one more time for 30 minutes.

Place the loaves in a preheated 350 degree oven and bake for 30 minutes. Take the bread out of the loaf pans immediately (it should give a nice hollow thump if it's done). Like all breads, this one is really good hot out of the oven.

FRESH CORN CORNBREAD

makes 6-8 servings

2 1/2 cups cornmeal
1 tsp. salt
1/2 tsp. baking powder
1/2 tsp. baking soda
3 tbsp. honey
2 eggs
2 cups buttermilk (if you don't have any then you can sour regular milk
with a splash of vinegar, or you can substitute 1 cup regular milk and 1
cup plain yogurt)
1/4 cup oil or melted butter
1 tsp. cumin seeds
1 cup fresh corn kernels (canned or frozen are all right, too)

Preheat oven to 425 degrees. Sift the cornmeal, salt, baking powder
and soda together in one bowl. In another bowl mix the honey, eggs,
milk, and oil. Add the dry ingredients to the wet, stir in the corn and
cumin, and pour into a greased 8"x8" pyrex dish. Bake 20-25 minutes.

JALAPENO CHEESE CORN BREAD

makes 6-8 servings

3 tbsp. butter
3 tbsp. honey
1 1/2 cups corn meal
1 cup unbleached white flour
1 tbsp. baking powder
1/2 tsp. baking soda
1 egg
1 cup buttermilk
1 cup corn kernels (preferably from fresh corn)
1 cup grated hot pepper jack or cheddar cheese

Preheat oven to 350 degrees. Melt butter, stir in honey. Mix dry ingredients together. In a seperate bowl, beat together egg and buttermilk, stir in the melted butter/honey. Mix the dry with the wet ingredients, stir in the corn and cheese. Pour into a greased, floured 8"x8" baking pan. Bake for 30 minutes, until the top is golden brown. This is best served hot.

CORNBREAD-CHEESE PUDDING WITH FRESH HERBS

makes 8 servings

3 cups cornbread crumbs
1 cup corn kernels (fresh, canned, or frozen)
1 cup chopped fresh herbs: parsley, arugula, dill and/or basil
2 eggs
2 cups milk
1 tsp. salt
2 cups grated cheddar cheese

Preheat oven to 350 degrees. Grease a 8"x8" pyrex dish. Crumble corn-bread into it, then add the corn and the herbs. Beat eggs, milk, and salt, pour into pan. Sprinkle cheese over all, bake for 30 minutes. Serve hot.

BASIC CREPES

3 eggs
1/2 cup cold water
1 cup milk, half-and-half, or a combination of both
1 1/2 cups unbleached white flour, sifted
1 tbsp. canola oil
1/2 tsp. salt
butter for greasing the crêpe pan (< 1 stick)

You really should have a crêpe pan for making these, the task will be made much easier. If you don't, then a shallow-sided heavy frying pan, preferably non-stick, will do. Beat eggs, water, and milk together. Whisk in the flour, oil, and salt, beat till smooth. Allow the batter to rest for an hour in the refrigerator (if you're pressed for time, you can skip this step).

Heat your crêpe or frying pan and melt a pat of butter in it, swirling it around. When the butter stops bubbling, pour a small amount (I start with a 1/2 ladleful) of batter into the pan. Tilt the pan around quickly to evenly spread the batter over it. Cook a minute or two, until the edges start to curl up, then flip the crêpe over and cook on the other side, about a minute. It should be golden brown on both sides. Slide the crêpe onto a plate and repeat the process till the batter is gone. You can stack the crêpes on top of each other till you are ready to fill them. They also freeze well; simply seperate each crêpe with a piece of waxed paper, and store them, stacked and wrapped, in your freezer. To use them, just defrost.

CORN, BASIL, AND CHEESE FILLING FOR CREPES

makes 12 crêpes

3 tbsp. butter
2 shallots, minced
2 cloves garlic, minced
2 tbsp. flour
1 cup milk or half-and half
1 1/2 cups grated cheddar
1 cup corn (fresh or canned)
2 carrots, peeled and sliced thinly
1 celery stalk, sliced thinly
salt, pepper to taste
1 cup minced fresh basil
12 crêpes

In medium-sized heavy pot, heat butter. Add shallots and garlic and sauté 5 minutes. Add flour and whisk till it gets toasty brown. Whisk in the milk or cream and stir till thickened, about 10 minutes. Add remaining ingredients, except basil, and simmer over medium-low heat, stirring occasionally, until the vegetables are just cooked, about 10 minutes.

To make crêpes: Lay out a (warm or room temperature) crêpe in front of you. Place a few spoonsful of the filling in a stripe down the middle of the crêpe, sprinkle with some fresh basil. Roll up the crêpe and place on a plate or platter. If you're making these in advance of serving, then make all the crêpes, wrap and refrigerate. Warm in a 300 degree oven, covered, for 15 minutes, before serving.

These look nice when dusted with a little paprika on top.

CARROT-SCALLION QUICHE WITH BUTTERMILK

makes 1 quiche

3 eggs
1 1/2 cups buttermilk
1/2 lb. grated hard cheese, such as monterey jack, cheddar, and/or
swiss
6 large carrots, grated
6 scallions, sliced thinly
2 tsps. cumin seeds
1 tsp. thyme
1/2 tsp. salt
pinch pepper
1 unbaked quiche shell

Preheat oven to 375 degrees. In a large mixing bowl, whisk the eggs
for a minute and add the buttermilk; whisk together a minute more. Stir
in cheese(s) and spices. Scatter the grated carrots and the scallions
evenly in the pie shell. Pour in the buttermilk mixture. Bake for 40-45
minutes, till top is golden brown.

EGGPLANT QUICHE

makes 1 quiche (6-8 servings)

crust:
1/2 cup (1 stick) butter or margarine
1 1/2 cups unbleached white flour
1 tsp. salt
up to 1/4 cup ice water

fried eggplant:
1 medium eggplant, sliced into 1/2" rounds
1 cup whole wheat flour
1 tsp. each: oregano, thyme, dill, rosemary
2 eggs
olive oil for shallow frying

the rest of the pie:
1 cup tomato sauce
1 1/2 cups grated cheddar cheese
4 eggs
1 cup milk or cream

Make the crust: In a food processor, beat the butter, flour, and salt, and add the water, a little at a time, until the dough forms a ball. When it does, wrap in plastic or waxed paper and refrigerate for 1/2 hour. Meanwhile...

Make the fried eggplant: In a large shallow bowl, stir the flour and spices together. In another bowl, beat the eggs. Heat 1" of oil in a large skillet. Dip the eggplant in the egg, then dredge it in flour, then fry until golden brown on each side. Drain on paper towels. Do all the eggplant this way. Now...

Make the pie: Roll out the chilled dough, place it in your quiche pan. Preheat oven to 375 degrees. Spread 1/2 the tomato sauce on the quiche crust, then lay 1/2 the eggplant slices on this. Spread the grated cheese evenly over the eggplant, then spread the remaining tomato sauce and lay the rest of the eggplant slices on top. Beat the eggs with the milk or cream, pour it over the quiche, and bake for 45-50 minutes.

ONION PIE

makes 1 pie, 6-8 servings

1 unbaked pie crust
1/3 cup butter
8 cups onions, sliced thinly
3 egg yolks
1/2 cup heavy cream
1 tbsp. caraway seeds
salt to taste
pinch nutmeg

Lay the pie crust in a pie tin and crimp with your fingers or a fork.
Preheat oven to 400 degrees. In large heavy skillet, melt butter. Add
onions and sauté 15 minutes, until soft and pale gold.

In a medium-sized bowl, beat yolks till they are thick and lemony.
Add cream and seasonings, mix well. Stir sauteéd onions into this,
pour into pie crust. Bake for 1/2 hour.

TOFU PIE WITH HERBS AND BLACK OLIVES
- NO DAIRY

makes 1 pie

unbaked pie shell
3 tbsp. olive oil
2 cloves garlic, minced
1 large red onion, quartered and sliced thinly
1 1/2 lbs mushrooms (any kind, but portobellos are good), sliced thinly
1 lb. spinach, rinsed and chopped coarsely
2 lbs. tofu, drained
1 tbsp. each: dried rosemary, dill, and thyme
1/2 tsp. salt
1 cup sliced black olives

Lay the pie shell in your pie dish and crimp with your fingers or a fork. Preheat oven to 350 degrees. Heat oil in a large skillet. Add onions and garlic, sauté 5 minutes. Add mushrooms and spinach, lower heat, cover, and cook until mushrooms are done, about 10-15 minutes. Place tofu in a food processor or blender and pureé. Place this in a bowl, mix in the sauteédvegetables, the seasonings, and the black olives, blend together well. Pour this into the pie crust and bake for 45 minutes.

CHESTNUT STUFFING, FOR SQUASH OR TURKEY

This dish is greatly enhanced by using a nice crusty bread as its base. The better the bread, the better the stuffing will be- go to the bakery and treat yourself to one of those big football-shaped loaves, brown and dusty with flour.

makes 1 quart, approximately

1 lb. chestnuts
1 large loaf of bread, preferably something whole wheat and crusty
4 tbsp. butter or olive oil
1 large onion, diced
5 cloves garlic, minced
2 lbs. mushrooms (shiitake, porcini, or oyster are best), sliced thinly
1 bunch celery, sliced thinly
1 tbsp. sage leaves, minced
salt, pepper to taste
2 cups vegetable stock (or water)

Prepare chestnuts: cut an "x" across the top of the chestnuts, place on a cookie sheet, and bake for 20 minutes at 350 degrees. Meanwhile, tear the bread into chunks, place in a large bowl. Heat the butter in a skillet, add the onion and garlic and sauté for 5 minutes. Add the mushrooms and sauté 10 minutes more. Place in the bowl with the bread and the remaining ingredients.

When the chestnuts are done, allow them to cool somewhat and peel them out of their shells. Chop into chunky pieces and put them in the bowl. Pour in the vegetable stock (or water) and mix the stuffing well, using your hands.

You can use this stuffing to stuff a bird, or for the vegetarians in your midst, stuff any kind of winter squash with this and make them (and you) happy. If you are stuffing squash, cut them in half, scoop out the seeds, and bake the squash halfway. Fill with stuffing, put the squash halves in a greased casserole dish, cover, and bake 15 minutes at 350 degrees. Take off the cover and bake 5 minutes more, till golden brown. Serve with cheese and/or tahini sauce on the side.

Soups

VEGETABLE STOCK

CALDO VERDE

CURRIED CAULIFLOWER SOUP WITH ALMONDS

COCONUT SOUP

CORN CHOWDER WITH TOASTED HAZELNUTS

CREAM OF BROCOLLI SOUP WITH BASIL

GARLIC, ASPARAGUS, AND WHITE BEAN SOUP

GOLDEN CHICKPEA-SQUASH SOUP

HEARTY POTATO-LEEK SOUP

HOT AND SOUR SOUP

INDIAN-STYLE COCONUT SOUP

LEEK-POTATO SOUP WITH BARLEY

LEMON-MISO SOUP WITH VEGETABLES

MINESTRONE

MULLIGATAWNY

MUSHROOM-BARLEY SOUP

NEW YEAR'S BEAN SOUP

ORANGE-CARROT SOUP WITH LENTILS

POTATO SOUP WITH INDIAN SPICES

SPINACH SOUP WITH GARLIC AND ROSEMARY

BUTTERNUT SQUASH SOUP WITH TARRAGON

SWEET AND SOUR LO MEIN NOODLE SOUP

TOFU WONTONS IN EGG DROP-SHIITAKE SOUP

TOMATO, BASIL, AND BARLEY SOUP

YELLOW SPLIT PEA SOUP WITH INDIAN SPICES

The Zen cook follows the middle way. We have faith that the soup is coming along- but we still check now and then.
                    -Bernard Glassman

   Soup. It's what we crave on a raw late-winter evening, preferably simmering on the stove all day, preferably made by mom. The myth of soup, that good ones take all day to make, is only that- a myth. Good ones can take as little as 20 minutes to prepare - the miso soups are great in this respect. Most soups can be prepared, from the time you start chopping the vegetables, to the time you serve up a steaming bowl to your family, in about an hour. Vegetable stock is one of the only time-consuming recipes in this chapter, because of its long simmer time. So make a lot of it and freeze it. If you don't have stock, and don't have the time to make it, you can always substitute water. Stock, in addition to putting to good use your vegetable odds and ends, gives clear soups more body, but it's not essential.

   Most soups improve on standing, so they are practical, too. There are lots of folks out there who make a big pot of soup on Sunday to enjoy during the week when they get home from work too late or tired to put a lot of effort into dinner. They bring home a fresh loaf from the bakery, toss a quick salad, heat the soup, and dinner's ready.

   If you've got some vegetables, some grain or pasta, some beans, and some herbs, you've got soup.

So let's go.

VEGETABLE STOCK

makes 1 gallon (about)

2 onions, peeled and halved
4 carrots, thickly sliced
4 stalks celery, thickly sliced
6 cloves garlic peeled
1 potato, cut into 2-inch cubes
3-4 outer cabbage leaves
bunch parsley
10 peppercorns
optional: various vegetable cuttings from other cooking projects-
potato peels, brocolli stalks, cabbage cores, etc.
1 tbsp. salt.

In a large pot, place all the ingredients and 2 gallons water. Bring to a boil, lower heat, and simmer, uncovered, for 3-4 hours. Strain in a colander. Taste it. If it is weak, return it to the pot and simmer some more until it is the strength you want it. This keeps in the refrigerator for 3-4 days, and it freezes well.

CALDO VERDE

Kale renders this soup a pretty pale green color. Also called "vitamin C soup" in my family, I make it when someone's coming down with a cold.

serves 6-8

1 1/2 lbs. kale, chopped
3 or more cloves garlic- this should be garlicky; the more, the better
4 large potatoes, peeled and cut into chunks
up to 1 gallon vegetable broth (optional)
salt, pepper to taste

In a large pot, bring 2 cups vegetable broth (or water) to a boil. Add garlic, potatoes, and kale. Cover and cook until all ingredients are soft, about 15 minutes. Place into a food processor and pureé until smooth. Bring remaining vegetable broth (or water) to a boil in the same pot, stir in the contents of the food processor, mix well. Simmer for 10 minutes, season to taste, and serve.

CURRIED CAULIFLOWER SOUP WITH ALMONDS

serves 4-6

3 tbsp. canola oil
4 cloves garlic, minced
2 onions, diced
1 head cauliflower, broken into florets
1/2 cup white basmati rice
2 cups soy, rice, or cow milk
1 tsp. coriander powder
1 tbsp. (or to taste) curry powder
1/2 tsp. salt
1 cup slivered toasted almonds
1/2 cup fresh coriander leaves

Heat oil in a soup pot. Add onion and garlic. Sauté 5 minutes, till onion is soft. Add cauliflower, rice, and 2 cups water, bring to a boil, lower heat to medium-low. Cover pot and cook for 10 minutes, till the cauliflower is cooked. Add milk, seasonings, and almonds, and simmer 10 more minutes. Adjust for seasonings, toss in the coriander leaves and serve.

COCONUT SOUP

makes 6-8 servings

1 medium onion
1 head cauliflower
3 stalks celery
1 large carrot
1 small apple, peeled and cored
1/2 cup dried unsweetened coconut
1 can (16 oz.) coconut milk
1 cup coriander leaves
1 tsp. garam masala (an Indian spice mixture available at Indian
markets. Omit if you don't have any; there's no substitute)
1/2 tsp. curry powder
salt, pepper to taste

Cut vegetables and apple into chunks. Bring 1 quart water to a boil in a heavy soup pot. Add vegetables and cook, covered, over medium-high heat, until the vegetables are soft, about 15 minutes. Place the contents of the pot into a food processor or blender and pureé. Return the pureé to the pot and stir in the remaining ingredients with 1 cup water. Bring to a boil, reduce heat, and simmer 5-10 minutes. Check for seasonings and serve.

Optional- to make this a more substantial soup, like a meal in itself, serve the soup with white basmati rice stirred in.

CORN CHOWDER WITH TOASTED HAZELNUTS

This variation on the chowder theme happened when I toasted way too many hazelnuts for a cheesecake I was making. I threw them into the soup simmering on the stove, and experienced one of those culinary epiphanies that makes cooking so rewarding. If you're short of hazelnuts, this soup is great without them, but try it at least once with them.

serves 6-8

3 tbsp. olive oil
1 large onion, quartered and sliced thinly
2 cloves garlic, minced
3 cups corn kernels (referably fresh)
2 cups milk (or 1/2 & 1/2, or a combination of both)
2 cups vegetable stock (or water)
2 carrots, peeled and sliced thinly
3 stalks celery, sliced thinly
salt, pepper to taste
1/2 cup minced parsley
1 cup toasted hazelnuts, ground

Heat oil in a soup pot. Add onion and garlic, sauté 5 minutes. Add corn, milk, stock (or water), carrots, and celery. Bring to a boil, lower heat, cover (place the lid slightly askew so the steam can escape), and simmer 1/2 hour. Season to taste, stir in the parsley and ground hazelnuts, and serve.

CREAM OF BROCOLLI SOUP WITH BASIL

serves 6-8

2 tbsp. olive oil
1 large onion, quartered and sliced
3 cloves garlic
1 quart vegetable stock (or water)
2 heads brocolli, cut up into chunks
2 medium white potatoes, cut into 1" dice
3 cups fresh basil leaves
1 cup half-and -half or cream
salt. pepper to taste

Heat oil in a soup pot, add onion and garlic, sauté 5 minutes. Add vegetable stock (or water), bring to a boil, add brocolli and potatoes. Lower heat to medium, and simmer 15 minutes, till the vegetables are soft. Put into a food processor, add the basil, and pureé till smooth. Return to pot, add cream and enough water to make it the consistency of your liking, and simmer 10 more minutes, till heated through. Season to taste and serve.

GARLIC, ASPARAGUS, AND WHITE BEAN SOUP

A hearty little soup I always look forward to when spring comes and asparagus returns to the market.

serves 6-8

3 tbsp. olive oil
6 cloves garlic (or more), minced
3 cups cooked cannelloni (or other white) bean
1 quart vegetable stock (or water)
1 lb. asparagus, cut into 1" pieces
salt, pepper to taste

Heat oil in a soup pot. Add garlic and sauté till it's golden brown, about 10 minutes. Add beans and stock (or water), bring to a boil, add the asparagus. Lower heat and simmer 20 minutes, till the asparagus is cooked. Season and serve. You may add water, if you like a thinner soup, or allow some of the water to steam off, if you like it thick.

GOLDEN CHICKPEA-SQUASH SOUP

serves 8

2 cups cooked chickpeas
1 small acorn squash, peeled, seeded, cubed, and steamed until
just done (about 20 minutes)
3 tbsp. butter or oil
1 tbsp. cumin seeds
1 large onion, quartered and sliced thinly
4 cloves garlic, minced
1 tsp. curry powder
1 tsp. ground coriader
1 tsp. ground cardamon
salt to taste
handful coriander leaves, torn into little leaflets

Pureé chickpeas and squash together. In a soup pot, heat the
shortening. Add cumin seeds, onion, and garlic, sauté 10 minutes. Add
chickpea/squash pureé, 1 quart water, and spices.

Cook over medium heat, partially covered, for 1/2 hour. Add more
water if you like a thinner consistency. Before serving, sprinkle some
coriander leaves into each bowl.

This soup improves on standing- make it a few days in advance, if you like.

HEARTY POTATO-LEEK SOUP

serves 6

2 large leeks
1 can (18 oz.) red kidney beans, drained and rinsed
3 cloves garlic
4 medium red potatoes, diced into 1" cubes
1 cup small pasta, such as orzo, ditalini, macaroni
salt, pepper to taste

To prepare leeks: peel off the tough outer layer. Cut off the green tops. Slice out the white inner layers, cut these into 2" slices, place in a colander, and rinse well. Put the kidney beans and garlic in a food processor or blender and pureé. Bring 1 1/2 quarts water to a boil. Add pureéd beans and garlic, leeks and potatoes, lower heat. Simmer 20 minutes, partially covered, over medium heat. Add pasta, salt, and pepper, and cook 15 minutes more, till the pasta is done.

HOT AND SOUR SOUP

serves 6

3 tbsp. sesame oil
2 cloves garlic, minced
1" piece ginger, minced
1 large onion, diced
up to 2 quarts vegetable stock (or water)
4 carrots, sliced thinly
4 stalks celery, sliced thinly
1 cup shiitake or oyster mushrooms (fresh), sliced thinly
8 oz. firm tofu, cut into 1/2" dice
2 stalks lemon grass, the hard outer leaves take off, the inner part minced
jalapeno peppers (to taste), minced
1/4 cup lemon juice
1/2 cup hoisin sauce (available at health food stores and oriental markets)
1 tsp. (or more) cayenne powder
1 tbsp. tamari

In a large soup pot, heat oil. Add garlic, ginger, and onion, sauté 10 minutes.
Add vegetable stock (or water), bring to a boil. Add the remaining ingredients, bring to a boil again. Immediately lower heat to medium-low, cover, and simmer for 20 minutes, till the vegetables are cooked. Check for seasonings and serve.

INDIAN-STYLE COCONUT SOUP

makes 6 servings

2 tbsp. butter or oil
1 2" piece ginger, minced
3 cloves garlic, minced
1 tbsp. fennel seeds
1 tbsp. cumin seeds
2 16-oz. cans coconut milk
3 stalks celery, sliced very thinly
1/2 c. unsweetened coconut, not toasted
1/2 c. unsweetened coconut, toasted
1/2 tsp. curry powder (or to taste)
1 tsp. salt
1/2 cup fresh coriander leaves

Heat oil in your soup pot. Add ginger, garlic, fennel and cumin seeds, sauté till brown, 5-10 minutes. Stir in coconut milk, celery, and untoasted coconut, bring to a boil, lower heat, cover, and simmer 10 minutes. Add toasted coconut, curry, and salt, simmer 5 more minutes. Serve with a few coriander leaves sprinkled on top of each bowl of soup.

LEEK-POTATO SOUP WITH BARLEY

serves6-8

3 quarts vegetable stock (or water)
5 large leeks
3 large potatoes, cut into 1" dice
1 tbsp. dried tarragon
1 cup barley
1 tbsp. (or to taste) tamari

Bring stock or water to a boil in a large soup pot. Prepare leeks: slice the inner white part of the leaves into 1" pieces and rinse thoroughly. When liquid is boiling, put in the remaining ingredients, bring to a boil again, lower heat to medium-low. Cover and simmer for 30 minutes. Season to taste and serve.

LEMON-MISO SOUP WITH VEGETABLES

serves 4-6

2 tbsp. (or to taste) tamari
1 large onion, quartered and sliced thinly
4 carrots, peeled and sliced thinly
2 potatoes, peeled and cut into 1" dice
1/2 lb. fresh mushrooms (shiitakes are good), sliced thinly
1 cup hijiki (dried seaweed)
1 cup cooked chickpeas
1/2 cup miso
1/2 cup lemon juice

Bring 1 gallon of water to a boil in your soup pot. Add tamari, onion, carrots, potatoes, mushrooms, hijiki. Lower heat to a simmer, cover, and cook for 15 minutes, until the vegetables are soft. Add the chickpeas, miso, lemon juice; stir. Let simmer (don't let it boil- you'll kill the liveliness of the miso) for 10 more minutes, adjust for seasonings, and serve.

MINESTRONE

Minestrone, the classic "kitchen sink" soup, is a tomato-based soup that includes beans, pasta, and vegetables. An ideal way to use up those little bits of pasta you have in the boxes lined up in your pantry, and the odds and ends in your vegetable crisper.

makes 8 servings

1/4 cup olive oil
1 large onion, quartered and sliced thinly
4 cloves garlic, minced
1 gallon vegetable stock (or use water and vegetarian soup base powder)
3 lbs. fresh tomatoes, chopped
1 lb. mushrooms, sliced thinly
6 carrots, peeled and sliced thinly
4 stalks celery, sliced thinly
2 tbsp. each: dried oregano, thyme, tarragon, rosemary
salt to taste
2 cups cooked kidney beans (or white beans)
1 lb. small pasta, such as macaroni, ditallini, or orzo

Heat oil in your soup pot and add the onion and garlic, sauté 10 minutes. Add the vegetable stock (or water) and the remaining ingredients, except the beans and pasta. Bring to a boil, lower heat, and simmer, uncovered, for 1/2 hour. Add the beans, raise the heat to a boil, add the pasta. Cook until the pasta is done, about 10 minutes. Check for seasonings and serve.

MULLIGATAWNY

serves 8-10

3 tbsp. oil
1 large onion, chopped
3 cloves garlic, minced
1 green pepper, chopped
4 stalks celery, cut into 1" slices
4 carrots, peeled and sliced
1 large cooking apple (such as macoun or mackintosh), cored and
chopped
3 cups cooked chickpeas
1 tsp. salt
1 tbsp. curry powder
1 tsp. ground coriander
coriander leaves, for garnish

Heat oil in your soup pot. Add onion and garlic, sauté 5 minutes.
Add pepper, celery, carrots, apple, and 2 cups water, cover and cook
for 10 minutes. Add remaining ingredients, cook 5 minutes more.
Allow to cool somewhat (for easier handling) and put in a food
processor. Pureé and return to pot. Add enough water to make it the
consistency you'd like, simmer for 10 minutes. Serve with some
coriander leaves sprinkled over the top.

MUSHROOM-BARLEY SOUP

serves 6-8

3 tbsp. olive oil
1 large onion, quartered and sliced thinly
3 cloves garlic, minced
2 lbs. mushrooms, sliced thinly
1/4 cup tamari
1/4 cup rice vinegar
1 1/2 qts. vegetable stock (or water)
2 cups dried barley
3 tbsp. dried tarragon
salt, pepper to taste

Heat oil in your soup pot. Add onions and garlic and cook over medium heat for 5 minutes. Stir in mushrooms and sauté for 5 minutes. Add tamari and rice vinegar and stir. Cover the pot and simmer for 10 minutes, stirring occasionally. Add water or stock and barley and bring to a boil. Lower heat right away, cover the pot halfway, and simmer until the barley is done, about 20 minutes. Add the rest of the spices and serve.

NEW YEAR'S BEAN SOUP

Many European cultures recommend, if not require, the eating of beans on New Year's Eve to ensure good luck for the next year. My family was not one to buck this tradition, and so we dined on bean soup at midnight on New Year's Eve. This is my mother's recipe, with one omission: the beef short ribs that would simmer along with the beans and sauerkraut. This vegetarian version puts forth the hope that the cows have a good year, too.

serves 8

2 cups dried pinto beans
2 tbsp. shortening
3 cloves garlic, minced
2 large onions, quartered and sliced thinly
3 tbsp. caraway seeds
salt and pepper to taste
1 cup sauerkraut

garnishes:
sour cream
horseradish
more sauerkraut

Bring 1 gallon of water to a boil and cook the beans; it should take an hour or so. Drain and rinse. In a heavy-duty soup pot, heat the shortening. Add the onions and garlic, sauté 10 minutes, till pale gold in color. Add 2 quarts of water, the cooked beans, caraway seeds, seasonings, and sauerkraut. Simmer, partially covered, for 1/2 hour.

Serve with the garnishes on the side; this is good with a little bit of each stirred in.

ORANGE-CARROT SOUP WITH LENTILS

The orange peel in this soup is a subtle surprise.

makes 6-8 servings

2 tbsp. canola oil
1 large onion, chopped
1 tbsp. fennel seeds
1 lb. carrots, sliced thinly
peel of 1/2 orange
4 stalks celery, sliced thinly
2 cups salmon or red lentils, soaked at least 1 hour
salt, pepper to taste

Heat oil in a heavy-duty soup pot. Add onions and fennel seeds and sauté 5 minutes. Add remaining ingredients and 3 quarts water. Bring to a boil, lower heat to medium-low, cover, and simmer for 45 minutes-1 hour, until the lentils are cooked. You may need to add a little more water if you like your soup thin; if you like it thick take the cover off and let the cooking liquid steam off. Check for seasonings and serve.

POTATO SOUP WITH INDIAN SPICES

serves 6

3 tbsp. butter
1 tbsp. each: coriander, cumin, and black mustard seeds
2" piece of ginger, minced
3 cloves garlic, minced
1 large onion, diced
1/2 cup white basmati rice (uncooked)
4 medium white potatoes, diced
1 cup coconut milk
1/2 tsp. cinnamon
salt to taste
bunch fresh coriander leaves, torn into small pieces (for garnish)

Melt the butter in your soup pot. Add the seeds, stir around for a minute or two, till they start to pop, then add the ginger, garlic, and onion. Lower heat and sauté for 10 minutes, until the onion is nicely browned. Add 3 quarts water and bring to a boil. Lower heat and add the potatoes, rice, coconut milk, and the cinnamon. Simmer, partially covered, for 20 minutes, until the potatoes and rice are cooked. Check for seasonings and serve each bowl with a handful of coriander leaves tossed on top.

SPINACH SOUP WITH GARLIC AND ROSEMARY

serves 6-8

3 tbsp. olive oil
1 large onion, choppped
4-6 cloves garlic, minced
3 medium potatoes, cubed
2 lbs. spinach, rinsed and drained (fresh or frozen)
1 lb. tofu, cubed
3 tbsp. fresh rosemary leaves (or use dried)
1/2 cup miso
salt to taste

Heat oil in soup pot. Add onions and garlic, sauté 5 minutes. Add 1 quart water, bring to a boil, and add the potatoes, spinach, tofu, and rosemary. Lower heat, cover, and simmer till the potatoes are cooked, about 20 minutes. Pureé this in a food processor, then return it to the soup pot. Add 1 more quart water (adjust amount to how thick you like your soup), bring to a boil, lower heat immediately to medium. Stir in the miso, mix well, and serve.

BUTTERNUT SQUASH SOUP WITH TARRAGON

makes 6-8 servings

1 medium-sized butternut squash
3 tbsp. oil
1 large onion, quartered and sliced thinly
3 cloves garlic, minced
3 tbsp. dried tarragon
2 cups rice, soy, or cow's milk
2 tsp. paprika
salt, pepper to taste

Peel squash, cut in half, and scoop out seeds. Cut into chunks. Bring 1 quart water to a boil in a heavy pot. Put in the squash and cook, covered, until soft; about 20 minutes. Place the cooked squash into a food processor or blender and pureé, saving the liquid. Heat oil in your soup pot, add garlic and onion and sauté for 5 minutes. Add squash, the saved liquid, and the remaining ingredients. Simmer over medium heat for 1/2 hour, partially covered. Adjust for seasonings and serve.

SWEET AND SOUR LO MEIN NOODLE SOUP

serves 8

1 gallon vegetable stock (or water)
2" piece of ginger, minced
1 medium onion, quartered and sliced thinly
2 carrots, peeled and sliced thinly
1 large portobello mushroom, cut in half andf sliced thinly
1/2 head napa cabbage, sliced thinly
1 stalk lemon grass, minced
1/2 cup rice vinegar
1/4 cup sugar
12 oz. dried lo mein noodles
3 tbsp. tamari (or to taste)

Bring vegetable stock (or water) to a boil. Add the remaining ingredients except the noodles and tamari. Bring to a boil again, lower heat to medium, partially cover, and cook until the vegetables are just done, about 20 minutes. Add the noodles and tamari, cook 10 minutes more, until the noodles are done. Season to taste and serve.

TOFU WONTONS IN EGG DROP-SHIITAKE SOUP

serves 8-10

wontons:
3 tbsp. sesame oil
1/4 cup minced ginger
1 medium onion, chopped
1 red pepper, diced very small
1 cup mushrooms, diced very small
1 carrot, diced very small
1 lb. extra firm tofu, drained and crumbled
2 tbsp. tamari
20 wonton skins
1 egg

Heat oil in a heavy skillet. Add ginger and onion, sauté 5 minutes. Add pepper, mushrooms, and carrot, sauté till the vegetables are cooked and the liquid is steamed off, about 15 minutes. Add the crumbled tofu and the tamari, cook 5 minutes more, till the ingredients are thoroughly mixed.

Make the wontons: Beat the egg in a small dish. Bring 1 gallon of water to a boil. Lay out a wonton skin in front of you, brush the edge with egg, then place 2 tablespoons of tofu mixture in the center of the wonton skin. Bring the edges of the skin over to form a triangle, press the edges together firmly and thoroughly, so no filling can leak out. Bend the triangle in half again, carefully. Repeat till all the wontons are done, then put them into the boiling water. Cook for 5 minutes, then remove them from the water (with a slotted spoon). They are now ready to place in soup.

egg drop soup:

1 gallon vegetable stock (or water)
3 tbsp. miso
2 tbsp. minced lemon grass
3 tbsp. rice vinegar
1 cups fresh shiitake mushrooms, sliced very thinly
1 egg, beaten (use the remaining egg from the wontons)

Place all ingredients, except egg, into a soup pot and bring to a boil. When it boils, lower heat, and simmer 5 minutes. Stir in egg, cook 5 minutes more, till the soup achieves its egg-drop-soup look. Stir in the wontons and serve.

TOMATO, BASIL, AND BARLEY SOUP

serves6-8

3 tbsp. butter or olive oil
1 large onion, chopped
3 cloves garlic, minced
1 gallon vegetable stock (or water)
2 lbs. tomatoes, chopped
1 cup pearled barley
1 cup basil leaves, chopped
salt, pepper to taste

Heat shortening in your soup pot. Add onion and garlic, sauté till brown, 5-10 minutes. Add tomatoes and stock (or water), bring to a boil. Add barley, stir, lower heat to medium, and cook 30 minutes, partially covered, till barley is done. Season to taste, and toss in the basil leaves just before serving.

YELLOW SPLIT PEA SOUP WITH INDIAN SPICES

serves 6-8

3 tbsp. canola oil or butter
2 tbsp. each: brown mustard seeds, cumin seeds, and coriander seeds
2" cube of ginger (or more), minced
1 large onion, chopped
2 cups yellow split peas
1 1/2 quarts vegetable stock (or water)
3-4 carrots, sliced thinly
1 bunch parsley, minced
salt, pepper to taste
1/2 cup coriander leaves (optional)

Heat shortening in your soup pot. Add spices, stir around a moment till they begin to pop. Immediately stir in the ginger and onion, sauté a moment, then lower heat, cover, and cook 5 minutes, till the onions are soft (stir once or twice to keep from burning). Add split peas, stock (or water), and carrots. Raise heat to medium-high, cover, and cook till peas are done, about 45 minutes. Toss in parsley, season to taste. If you are using coriander, stir a little into each bowl when serving.

Stews, Casseroles, Hot Dishes

AFRICAN-STYLE SPINACH AND KIDNEY BEAN STEW
BLACK BEAN CHILI WITH SPINACH
BROCOLLI, TOFU, GREENS, GARLIC WITH COCONUT & CORIANDER
CARIBBEAN-STYLE VEGETABLE STEW WITH PEANUT SAUCE
INDIAN-STYLE RED LENTILS WITH VEGETABLES
KABULI CHOLE
RATATOUILLE
SWEET POTATO STEW WITH BLACK BEANS AND TOFU
TOFU STROGANOFF
TOFU WITH GREEN CURRY AND COCONUT SAUCE
TOFU WITH WINTER VEGETABLES & UDON NOODLES
VEGETABLE STEW WITH ETHIOPIAN SPICES
BAKED FETTUCINE ALFREDO WITH SUNDRIED TOMATO PESTO
CABBAGE ROLLS WITH SPINACH-CASHEW FILLING
STRATA OF EGGPLANT, TUBETTI, AND SPINACH CREAM
MANICOTTI WITH SPINACH-HERB FILLING
PEPPERS STUFFED WITH RED LENTILS AND RICE FLORENTINE
RICE CASSEROLE
SCALLOPED POTATO-SPICED RICE-CHEESE STRATA
SQUASH WITH SPINACH-RICE STUFFING
SUMMER SQUASH STUFFED WITH SESAME-SEASONED TOFU
&VEGETABLES AND TAHINI SAUCE
SWEET CORN CHILAQUILES W/TOMATILLO SAUCE
SWISS CHARD LEAVES STUFFED WITH HAZELNUTS AND RICE WITH
BASIL SAUCE
CURRIED RICE PILAF WITH COCONUT MILK
CURRIED TEMPEH STIR-FRY WITH RICE NOODLES
FETTUCINE WITH SHIITAKE MUSHROOMS AND BECHAMEL SAUCE
GINGER-BAKED (OR GRILLED) TOFU
KASHA, CARROTS, CARAWAY, & CASHEWS
PEANUTTY-GINGERY TOFU CUTLETS
PHYLLO TRIANGLES WITH SPINACH-PINE NUT-TOFU FILLING (VEGAN)
PHYLLO TRIANGLES FILLED WITH PANEER, CHARD, AND INDIAN
SPICES
RED CHILI RICE
SMOKED MOZZARELLA, BROWN BASMATI, AND HAZELNUT LOAF
SPINACH-ALMOND PILAF
TOASTED RICE WITH GARLIC
TOFU "MEATBALLS" FOR PASTA DISHES

Eating is an aspect of civilization. The way we grow our food, the kind of food we eat, and the way we eat it has much to do with civilization because the choices we make can bring about peace and relieve suffering.

-Thich Nhat Hanh

The recipes in this section are intended to be the central dish around which a meal is based. Some are inspired by the Italian genius for combining pasta, cheese, and vegetables; others by the Asian penchant for stir-frying vegetables and tofu and using herbs and coconut milk as a flavor enhancer. Also appearing on our culinary tour are Chilaquiles from Mexico, stuffed cabbage from eastern Europe, and hearty stews from Africa.

There is a world traveller living inside of me, and she has been frustrated by the outside of me not taking her on nearly enough adventures in the big world. We have visited only 3 of the 7 continents available to us. So far. But we have travelled the world via our taste buds. I give thanks to the many foreign writers of cookbooks who have shared the culinary arts of their kitchens with Americans. Cookbooks have been my teachers. The books of Madhur Jaffrey have been especially instuctional for me- she is an Indian writer, actress, and restaurateur, and has written many books on Indian and Asian cuisine. I highly recommend any and all of her books, if you are wont to delve more deeply into the joys of Asian cooking.

And here, a word about vegetables. People often assume I only use organic produce in my cooking. I was once an organic vegetable gardener, and have worked in greenhouses as the organic plantsman(woman?) on the staff, and so it is thought that I am a purist on such things. And yes, I am, as much as I can. But I am also a woman living in 21st century America. Striking a balance between the desire to live off the land and as lightly on the earth as possible, and the necessity of driving a car, heating my house with oil, and feeding my boys what they like- including Big Macs and steaks- is the challenge of thoughtful people in this society, of which I am one. When I am at the supermarket, I go to the organic section and purchase as much as I can from there. But if what I want isn't in that department, I'll move over to the conventional section. I am thrilled that most supermarkets carry organic fruits and vegetables now; I believe in voting with my dollar, so I buy organics at the A&P. I also buy them at the local co-op (which isn't so local for me- it's 25 miles away). And in the summer, there are vegetable stands galore out where I live in the sticks; I like those best of all. I love getting my vegetables from the source. Farmer's markets abound in the cities in summer and fall, so you urban folk aren't lacking in fresh fare from the fields, either. And it is important to support the small farmers who sell their goods at the markets. Family farms are being swallowed up by corporate agribusinesses; their work is necessary to maintain the little diversity in agriculture we still have.

Most of the meals I make, for home and catering, combine conventional and organic ingredients. It is never lost on me that the pretty stack of , say, conventionally grown red peppers was cultivated in a field fertilized by chemicals, de-bugged by pesticides, and harvested by migrant workers treated to substandard wages and terrible working conditions. There is little I can do about this paradox of beauty sprouting from the fields of greed and ignorance. I can write to my legislators, I can buy organic when possible. Those are things that I can do. What I must do, though, is to accept this world on its own terms. I only have control over my own actions, no one else's. And my action is to put love into the food I make. I am grateful for the red pepper I am about to slice, I am grateful to those who I slice it for, and I am grateful to those who grew and picked and delivered it for me to buy.

The Vietnamese Zen master Thich Nhat Hanh calls this "inter-being", and his mission as a peace maker is to remind us that everything is connected. My red pepper is made of soil, herbicide, sweat, chlorophyll, tractor diesel, sunlight. I can choose to be oppressed by the complex nature of life in society now, or I can choose gratitude for being given the opportunity to have a choice at all. Most days, I choose gratitude. I choose love.

AFRICAN-STYLE SPINACH AND KIDNEY BEAN STEW

In West Africa, peanuts are one of the largest cash crops. Peanuts and peanut oil are widely used in African cuisine. So are hot peppers. You can omit the hot peppers, and this stew will be fine. But if you like peppers- go for it! They're great in this stew.

serves 6-8

3 tbsp. peanut oil (or use corn or canola oil)
1 large onion, chopped
4 cloves garlic, minced
minced chili peppers, to taste
1 28-oz. can crushed tomatoes
1 cup cooked kidney beans
2 lbs. fresh spinach, chopped
1/2 cup natural peanut butter
1/2 cup toasted peanuts, chopped
1 tsp. salt
1/2 tsp. pepper

Heat oil in a heavy-duty pot. Add onion, garlic, and the chili(s), if you're using them. Sauté 5 minutes. Add crushed tomatoes, 1/4 cup water, kidney beans, and spinach, and simmer over medium heat, stirring often, for 10 minutes. Stir in the peanuts and peanut butter, simmer a few minutes more, till the spinach is cooked. Season to taste and serve.

This is good with rice, or you can serve it with fufu. Fufu is the West African counterpart to rice, a starchy product made of pounded taro root. Hard to find except in African markets. I have successfully substituted mashed potatoes.

BLACK BEAN CHILI WITH SPINACH

One of the few vegetarian meals I could get my kids to eat, until they developed a dislike for the dreaded bean. Oh well, more for the grownups...

serves 8-10

2 cups dried black beans, rinsed and soaked for up to 12 hours (The longer you soak them, the less you have to boil them. If you don't have time to soak them, that's okay- just allow more time for cooking them.)
1/4 cup oil
2 onions, diced
5 cloves garlic, minced
3 tbsp. cumin seeds
2 green peppers, diced
1-3 jalapeno peppers, minced (optional)
3 tbsp. (or to taste) chili powder
2 28-oz. cans crushed tomatoes
1 cup TVP (textured vegetable protein), or 1 lb. firm tofu, crumbled
2 lbs. spinach, rinsed and chopped
1 tbsp. (or to taste) tamari
grated cheddar (optional)

Bring 1 gallon water to a boil, add the black beans, and simmer until almost done- about 1 hour. Drain. Meanwhile, in a large soup pot, heat oil. Add onions, garlic, and cumin seeds; sauté for 5 minutes. Add peppers and chili powder and sauté 5 minutes more. Stir in tomatoes, 1/2 cup water, and the t.v.p. or tofu. Stir and simmer for 10 minutes, add the beans and the spinach, stir. Simmer, covered, over medium-low heat for 1/2 hour. Check for seasonings, add the tamari, and serve.

This is good over rice, with grated cheddar sprinkled over the top. It's especially good made a few days in advance to allow the flavors to mellow.

BROCOLLI, TOFU, GREENS, GARLIC
WITH COCONUT & CORIANDER

Oyster sauce and rice vinegar are both available at Oriental markets. Oyster sauce isn't made with oysters in it, it is used to flavor oysters (and other things). There's really no substitute, so if you don't have oyster sauce, just omit it. In a pinch, rice vinegar can be faked by stirring in a teaspoon of sugar into cider vinegar.

serves 4-6

1/4 cup sesame oil (or use canola)
1 large onion, diced
4 cloves garlic, minced
2" piece of ginger, minced
1 lb. extra firm tofu, cut into 1" cubes
1/2 cup vegetable stock
2 tbsp. tamari
1/4 cup oyster sauce
1/4 cup rice vinegar
1/2 cup coconut milk
1 head brocolli, cut up
1 lb. mustard greens, chopped
1/4 cup cornstarch
1 cup coriander leaves, torn into small leaflets

Heat oil in a wok. Add onion, garlic, and ginger, sauté 5 minutes. Add tofu and sauté 5 minutes more. Add stock, tamari, oyster sauce, rice vinegar, and coconut milk, bring to a boil. Add the brocolli and mustard greens, cover, lower heat, and cook for 5-10 minutes, till the brocolli is just done. Dissolve the cornstarch in 2 tablespoons of water, mix into the wok, stirring until the liquid is thickened. Sprinkle the coriander leaves over the top and serve over rice or noodles.

CARIBBEAN-STYLE VEGETABLE STEW
WITH PEANUT SAUCE

The banana chutney in Chapter 2 makes a great accompaniment to this dish.

makes 6 servings

1 large head cauliflower, cut into serving-size chunks
1 eggplant, cut into 2" cubes
2 tbsp. corn, canola, or peanut oil
3 cloves garlic, minced
1 large onion, chopped
4 stalks celery, sliced thinly
1 28-oz. can crushed tomatoes
2 cups cooked squash or pumpkin, pureéd
3 carrots, sliced very thinly
1/2 cup chunky natural peanut butter
1/4 cup lime juice
1/4 cup cider vinegar
1 tsp. salt
1 tsp. cumin powder
cayenne powder, or minced hot peppers, to taste

Steam cauliflower and eggplant until just cooked. In a heavy-duty pot, heat oil. Add garlic and onion, sauté 5 minutes. Add celery, crushed tomatoes, cooked squash, and carrots. Stir and simmer over low heat, covered, for 20 minutes. Stir in the peanut butter, lime juice, vinegar, and seasonings, simmer 5 minutes more. Add the steamed vegetables, mix well, and serve. This is good with jasmine-scented white rice and some chili sauce on the side.

INDIAN-STYLE RED LENTILS WITH VEGETABLES

Dal is the name for any Indian dish made with lentils that is somewhere between a soup and a stew. That's what this is.

serves 6-8

2 cups salmon or red lentils (any kind of lentil is fine, I like these the best)
3 tbsp. butter or oil
1-2 tbsp. each: coriander seeds, black mustard seeds, cumin seeds
1 large onion, quartered and sliced
6 cloves garlic, minced
2" piece ginger, minced
any or all of these vegetables, enough to make 1 quart: brocolli florets, cauliflower pieces, sliced carrots, diced yams, diced potatoes, green beans
1 28-oz. can crushed tomatoes
2 tsp. (or to taste) curry powder
1 tsp. salt

Soak lentils at least an hour (this cuts down on cooking time) and simmer in 1 1/2 quarts water for 1/2 hour- 1 hour, until they are done. Drain. In a heavy soup pot, heat shortening and add seeds. Stir them around until they pop (be careful), this shouldn't take more than a minute. Immediately add the onion, garlic, and ginger. Lower heat to medium and cook for 10 minutes. Add the vegetables and 1/2 cup water, stir, cover, and simmer 10 minutes. Add the remaining ingredients and the drained lentils. Simmer over medium-low heat for 20 minutes, stirring occasionally. Add water if you like this soupier, uncover and allow the water to steam off if you like this thicker.

As a stew it is good served over basmati rice, or you could serve this as a soup. The flavors develop over time; this is good if made a few days in advance.

KABULI CHOLE

In my humble opinion, this is the best thing that you can do to a chickpea. A lot of chickpeas. It's one of those nutritious, delicious crowd-
pleasing meals you can make days before serve it (it's actually better
that way).

serves 6-8

1/4 cup butter or oil
6 cloves garlic, minced
2" piece ginger, minced
1 large onion, quartered and sliced thinly
2 tbsp. each: cumin, coriander, fennel, and black mustard seeds
4 large tomatoes, diced
4 green peppers, cut into 1" pieces
3 carrots, sliced thinly
1 small can (4 oz.) tomato paste
3 cups cooked chickpeas
1 tsp. salt
1 tsp. curry powder

Heat shortening in a heavy duty soup pot. Add garlic, ginger, onion,
and spice seeds, sauté 10 minutes. Add tomatoes, peppers, and carrots,
lower heat, cover, and simmer 15 minutes, stirring occasionally. Add the
tomato paste, chickpeas, salt, and curry powder. Cook, covered, 10
minutes more. You might need to add a little water- this should be like a
stew.

Serve with white basmati rice and a variety of chutneys for a nice
Indian-style meal. This is good when the flavors are allowed to mellow
for a few days, and it keeps well.

RATATOUILLE

serves 4-6

1/4 cup olive oil
1 large onion, chopped
4 cloves garlic, minced
3 green peppers, chopped
4 large tomatoes, chopped
1 medium eggplant, cut into 1" cubes
2 zucchinis or summer (crookneck) squash, cut in half and
sliced into 1/2" rounds
1 tbsp. each: dried oregano, thyme, marjoram, and dill weed
1/2 cup fresh parsley, minced
1 tsp. (to taste) salt

In medium soup pot, heat oil. Add onion and garlic and sauté for 10 minutes. Add peppers and tomatoes and sauté for 5 minutes. Lower heat to medium-low, add 1/4 cup water and remaining ingredients. Stir well, cover, and simmer for 30 minutes, till the eggplant is cooked. Adjust for seasonings and serve over rice or pasta.

SWEET POTATO STEW WITH BLACK BEANS AND TOFU

serves 6-8

3 tbsp. canola oil
2 tbsp. cumin seeds
1 large onion, chopped
2" piece of ginger, minced
2 cups tomato sauce
2 large tomatoes, chopped
2 large sweet potatoes, cut into 1" cubes
1 green pepper, chopped
1 cup tofu, crumbled
1 cup black beans, cooked
1tsp. each: ground cumin, coriander, and cardamon
1/2 tsp. cinnamon
salt to taste

Heat oil in a heavy-duty pot. Add cumin seeds, stir a minute till they brown, then add the ginger and onion and sauté 5 minutes. Lower heat and stir in the tomato sauce, tomatoes, sweet potatoes, and pepper. Add 1 cup water, cover, and simmer 15 minutes, till the potatoes are soft. Add tofu and spices, stir and simmer 5 minutes. Serve with rice or wide egg noodles.

TOFU STROGANOFF

serves 6

3 tbsp. olive oil
1 large onion, chopped finely
3 cloves garlic, minced
1 lb. fresh mushrooms, slices (portobellos or shiitakes are good)
2 lbs. extra-firm tofu, drained and cut into 1" cubes
2 green peppers, quartered and sliced thinly
2 cups tomato pureé
1 tbsp. each: dried thyme, oregano, dill weed, and marjoram
1 tsp. salt (to taste)
1 cup sour cream (or whole milk yogurt)

Heat oil in a heavy-duty pot. Add onion and garlic and sauté over medium heat until soft, about 10 minutes. Add mushrooms, tofu, and peppers, sauté for 10 minutes. Add tomato pureé, and spices, stir, and simmer until the ingredients are just cooked through, about 10 minutes. Add sour cream (or yogurt), mix well, and serve. This is good with white rice or served atop wide egg noodles.

TOFU WITH GREEN CURRY AND COCONUT SAUCE

This stew is dandy without the green curry, but if you've gone to Oriental markets and wondered what the heck you could make from the curry pastes you've seen in cans on the shelves, well, here's your chance to try one out. The green, red, and yellow curries each have their own distinct flavors. Green is pungent and very hot. If you add just a tiny bit to this stew, you'll give it the flavor of the green curry and not much heat. But if you like it hot, go for it!

serves 6-8

3 tbsp. sesame oil (or substitute canola oil)
1 tbsp. coriander seeds
5 cloves garlic, minced
1" piece ginger, minced
2-4 tbsp. green curry (to taste)
1 large tomato, chopped
4 green peppers, quartered and sliced
2 stalks celery, sliced thinly
1 cup (8 oz.) coconut milk
2 lbs. extra firm tofu, drained and cut into 1" cubes
tamari to taste
1 cup coriander leaves, chopped

Heat oil in a large skillet or wok. Add coriander seeds, garlic, and ginger, sauté 10 minutes, till garlic is golden brown. Add green curry, tomato, peppers, and celery, sauté 5 minutes. Add coconut milk, tofu, and tamari; stir, cover, and simmer for 10 minutes over medium heat. Toss in coriander leaves, stir one more time and serve. This is good with jasmine-scented white rice.

TOFU WITH WINTER VEGETABLES & UDON NOODLES

Udon are Japanese whole wheat noodles, they are usually flat and somewhat thick. Cook them as you would pasta.

serves 8

3 tbsp. oil
3 cloves garlic, minced
1 large onion, quartered and cut into 1" cubes
1' piece of ginger, minced
3 cloves garlic, minced
1 cup each: sliced carrots; brocolli florets; diced winter squash
1 small sweet potato or yam, cut into 1/2" cubes
1 lb. mushrooms, sliced
1 bulb fennel, sliced thinly
2 lbs. extra firm tofu, drained and cut into 1" dice
2 cups vegetable stock (or water)
2 tbsp. (or to taste) tamari
3 tbsp. cornstarch, mixed with 1/4 cup water
2 pkgs. (1 lb.) udon noodles

Heat oil in a heavy-duty pot. Add garlic, onion, and ginger, sauté over medium-high heat 5 minutes. Add the vegetables and tofu and 1 cup water. Stir and simmer for 5 minutes. Add the remaining water and the tamari, cover, and cook over medium-low heat for 20 minutes, stirring occasionally. Stir in the cornstarch/water mixture, mix well. Bring 3 -4 quarts water to a boil, add udon noodles, cook 5 minutes, or until done. Drain. Add to the tofu stew, blend well, and serve.

VEGETABLE STEW WITH ETHIOPIAN SPICES

Haven't been to an Ethiopian restaurant yet? Well, what are you waiting for? The stews are among the finest in the world, and there are lots of vegetarian options. Best of all, you get to eat them with your hands-scooped up into injera, which is a sourdough flatbread ubiquitious to the Ethiopian table.

serves 6

1/4 cup butter
3 cloves garlic, minced
1 large onion, chopped
1 tbsp. each: cumin seeds, fennel seeds, mustard seeds
1/4 cup dried basil
1 tsp. turmeric
1/2 tsp. asafoetida
1/2 tsp. allspice
minced fresh chili or cayenne powder to taste (optional)
6 carrots, peeled and sliced
1 sweet potato, cut into 1" dice
2 potatoes, cut into 1" dice
1/2 lb. green beans
1 lb. fresh spinach, chopped
2 large fresh tomatoes, chopped, or 1 1/2 cups tomato sauce
1 small can (4 oz.) tomato paste
1 tsp. salt

Melt butter in a heavy-duty pot. Add garlic and onion, sauté 5 minutes. Lower heat to medium and add the spices, sauté 5 minutes more. Add the remaining ingredients, stir, and simmer over medium-low heat for 20 minutes, till the vegetables are just cooked. Check frequently and stir; you may need to add water. This should be served over rice, so you don't want it too runny, or too dry. The flavors in this stew develop on standing. It is best made a few days in advance, refrigerated, and heated up just before serving.

BAKED FETTUCINE ALFREDO
WITH SUNDRIED TOMATO PESTO

serves 6

1 lb. fettucine
1/2 cup sundried tomato pesto (see chapter 2)
1/2 cup parmesan cheese, grated
1/2 cup fontina (or Romano) cheese, grated
3/4 cup light cream
margarine or butter for greasing pan
1/2 cup (scant) bread crumbs

Preheat oven to 375 degrees. Cook fettucine, drain, return to pot with the sundried tomato pesto, the cheeses, and the cream. Grease an 8"x12" casserole dish, then line it with a layer of crumbs. Pour in the fettucine/pesto mixture, cover with foil, and bake 25 minutes. To serve, invert the casserole on a tray or plate, garnish with green or red lettuce leaves, and cut into squares.

CABBAGE ROLLS WITH SPINACH-CASHEW FILLING

My Hungarian mother's specialties were the wonderful dishes of her youth. Like most of us who were raised in Eastern European households, the smell of cooking cabbage brings back memories of my childhood. I can't imagine life without stuffed cabbage at least once a winter- my mom would stuff it with ground beef cooked with lots of onions and paprika. This recipe is my attempt at connecting with my heritage without eschewing my commitment to eating no meat.

makes 12 rolls

1 head cabbage

the sauce:
3 tbsp. oil
4 cloves garlic, minced
1 large onion, diced
1 28-oz. can crushed tomatoes, or 2 lbs. plum tomatoes, diced
1 can tomato paste
at least 1 tbsp. each: dried oregano, thyme, basil, marjoram
1-2 tbsp. paprika
1 tsp. salt
1 tsp. pepper

the filling:
2 lbs. spinach, rinsed
2 tbsp. oil
3 cloves garlic, minced
1 tsp.salt
1 tbsp. paprika
1 lb. tofu, drained
1 cup bread crumbs
1 cup cashews, toasted

2 cups grated mozzarella cheese (optional)

Pour boiling water over the cabbage. When the leaves are soft, cut off 12 outer leaves. Pour more boiling water over the leaves until they are pliable. (Save the remaining cabbage for another use.)

While cabbage is soaking, make the sauce: heat oil in a large skillet, add the garlic and onion. Sauté 10 minutes. Add the tomatoes and simmer for 5 minutes, stir in the tomato paste, herbs, and spices. Cook, stirring often, over medium heat for 15 minutes.

Make the filling: boil spinach, drain. Heat the oil in a small skillet, add the garlic, salt, and paprika, and sauté until the garlic is dark brown- 5-10 minutes. Place the spinach and tofu in a food processor or blender and pureé. Put this in a bowl with the sauteédgarlic, the bread crumbs, and the cashews. Place a few spoons of the filling in each cabbage leaf and roll up. Roll them eggroll-style, by placing the filling in the center of the leaf (with the thick part of the leaf at the top), folding over the 2 sides, then rolling towards you, keeping them tight.

In a casserole dish, spread 2/3 of the sauce. Lay the cabbage rolls in the dish, pour over the remaining sauce. If you are using cheese, sprinkle it over the rolls, cover with foil, and bake 20 minutes at 350 degrees. Remove the foil . Bake 10-15 minutes more, till the top is golden brown. If you are not using cheese, cover with foil and bake 30 minutes. This is good with rice or egg noodles on the side.

STRATA OF EGGPLANT, TUBETTI, AND SPINACH CREAM

serves 8-10

fried eggplant:
1 large eggplant, sliced into 1/2" rounds
1/2 c. whole wheat flour
olive oil for shallow frying

spinach cream:
3 tbsp. olive oil
1 large onion, chopped
3 cloves garlic, minced
2 lbs. spinach, chopped, steamed, and drained
1 tbsp. each: dried oregano, tatrragon, thyme, marjoram
1 cup sour cream

2 c. tubetti (or other tiny pasta)
2 c. good-quality (homemade is best) tomato sauce
1 c. grated mozzarella

To make eggplant: Dredge eggplant slices in flour and fry in a large skillet with an inch of oil in it, a few slices at a time. Drain on paper towels. (You can do this step up to a day ahead).

Make the spinach cream: in a large skillet, heat oil. Add the onion and garlic and sauté 5 minutes. Add the cooked spinach, sauté 5 minutes more. Stir in the herbs, salt, and sour cream.
Bring 1 quart water to a boil and cook the pasta. Drain.
Preheat oven to 350 degrees.

To make the strata, ladle tomato sauce on the bottom of a 9"x13" casserole dish. Lay 1/2 the eggplant slices down, then 1/2 the pasta, then 1/2 the spinach cream. Repeat the process; tomato sauce, then the remaining eggplant, pasta, and spinach cream. Carefully spread a layer of tomato sauce over all, then sprinkle the mozzarella over this. Cover with foil and bake 30 minutes. Take the foil off and bake 10 minutes more, till the cheese is golden brown.
Serve immediately.

MANICOTTI WITH SPINACH-HERB FILLING

makes 12 manicotti

3 tbsp. olive oil
3 cloves garlic, minced
1 medium onion, diced
2 lbs. spinach, rinsed
2 hardboiled eggs
1/2 cup ricotta cheese
1/2 cup cottage cheese
1/2 cup grated parmesan cheese
1 1/2 cups shredded mozzarella cheese
1/2 cup fresh basil leaves (or 3 tbsp. dried)
2 tbsp. each: dried oregano and thyme
11/2 tsp. pepper
1/2 tsp. salt
12 large manicotti shells
3 cups spaghetti sauce

Heat oil in a skillet. Add the garlic and onions and sauté until golden, about 10 minutes. Steam spinach, drain, and pureé in a food processor with the eggs. Put this into a bowl with the sauteédonion, the ricotta, cottage, parmesan cheeses, 1/2 cup mozzarella, herbs, and seasonings.
Mix well.
Preheat oven to 350 degrees.

Bring 1 gallon of water to a boil and cook the manicotti until they are done (they should be a little firm; don't overcook them).
Drain and stuff them with the filling.

Spread 1/2 the spaghetti sauce in the bottom of a casserole dish. Lay the manicotti on the sauce, spread the remaining sauce on the shells. Bake 45 minutes. Sprinkle the remaining 1 cup mozzarella over the shells 15 minutes before baking is done, return to oven. Serve when the cheese is melted and slightly toasted.

PEPPERS STUFFED WITH RED LENTILS AND RICE FLORENTINE

makes 8 peppers

1 cup red lentils
8 large red and/or green peppers
3 tbsp. olive oil
3 cloves garlic, minced
1 onion, chopped finely
1 lb. spinach, chopped
1 cup cooked rice
1" cube ginger, minced
4 cloves garlic, minced
1 large onion, chopped finely
1 cup bread crumbs
2 eggs
1 tbsp. each: dried oregano, thyme, tarragon
1/2 cup pine nuts
1 tsp. salt

Bring 2 1/2 cups water to a boil, add lentils, and cook over medium-high heat, uncovered, for 30 minutes, or until they are done. Cut off tops of the peppers and cut out the insides. Place in a greased baking dish. Heat the oil in a heavy skillet. Add the garlic, ginger, and onion, sauté 5 minutes. Add the spinach, sauté 5 more minutes. Place remaining ingredients in a bowl, add the cooked lentils and the vegetable mixture. Mix well.

Stuff the peppers with this mixture. Place in a casserole dish, cover with foil, and bake in a 375 degree oven for 25 minutes. Take off the foil and bake 5-10 more minutes, until the tops are golden brown. Serve with tahini-mustard sauce:

TAHINI-MUSTARD SAUCE

1/2 cup hot water
1/2 cup tahini
1/2 dijon mustard
dash tamari

Heat all ingredients in a small heavy pan. Whisk well to mix thoroughly.

RICE CASSEROLE

Got leftover rice and vegetables? Try this.

serves 6-8

1/4 cup sesame oil (any other oil is okay, but sesame adds a distinctive flavor)
1 tbsp. each: cumin, coriander, and black mustard seeds
1 large onion, chopped
2 cloves (or more) garlic, minced
up to 3 cups of any combination of these vegetables: chopped green peppers; carrots, sliced thinly; mushrooms, sliced thinly; brocolli florets (if you have leftover cooked vegetables, you can use those, too)
1 tbsp. tamari
3-4 cups cooked rice (brown, white, or a combination of both)
1 cup grated sharp cheddar cheese (optional)

Preheat oven to 350 degrees. Place all ingredients, except the cheese, in a bowl and mix well. Grease an 8"x12" casserole dish well, place the rice mixture in it. Cover with foil and bake for 30 minutes, take off the foil (if you're using cheese, sprinkle it on top at this point), and bake 10 minutes more.

SCALLOPED POTATO-SPICED RICE-CHEESE STRATA

serves 8-10

scalloped potatoes:
2 tbsp. oil
1 small onion, diced
3 cloves garlic, minced
3 large potatoes, cut in half and sliced 1/4" thick
1 tsp. salt
1 tsp. vinegar
1/2 cup cooking wine (optional; you can use water)

spiced rice:
1 1/2 cups white basmati rice
3 cups vegetable stock (or water)
1 cinnamon stick
1 tsp. cumin powder
1 tsp. fennel seeds
1 tsp. salt

1 cup grated sharp cheese
2 eggs
1 cup milk or half and half

Prepare potatoes: In a large skillet, heat oil. Add onion and garlic and sauté 5 minutes. Add potatoes, salt, vinegar, and wine (or water), cover, lower heat to medium. Cook 5 minutes, till the potatoes are about halfway done. Meanwhile, make the rice: bring the stock (or water) to a boil, add the rice and spices, stir, bring to a boil again. Cover and turn off the heat. Allow rice to steam for 15 minutes. It should be fluffed up in that time.

Preheat oven to 350 degrees . Grease a 9"x13" casserole dish. Carefully spoon the rice in (take out the cinnamon stick) and press it down firmly, flattening it to form a uniformly smooth "crust". Top it with the potatoes. Sprinkle the cheese evenly over this. Beat the eggs and milk (or cream) together, then pour it over the casserole. Cover with foil and bake 20 minutes. Take off the foil and bake 10 minutes more. Cut into squares and serve.

SQUASH WITH SPINACH-RICE STUFFING

Got leftover rice with no place to go? Stuff it in a squash half, make it happy.

serves 4

2 delicata or acorn squash
1 medium onion
1 clove garlic
2 lbs. spinach, steamed and drained of as much water as you can
2 cups cooked rice (brown basmati is good, but any kind will do)
1/2 cup pine nuts or chopped walnuts
1 cup grated parmesan cheese
1 tbsp. each: dried oregano, thyme, and dill weed
salt, pepper to taste
4 tsp. butter (optional)

Cut squash in half, scoop out the seeds, lay on a greased baking sheet, and bake at 350 degrees for 20 minutes. Meanwhile, place garlic and onion in a food processor (or blender) and mince. Add spinach, pureé till all ingredients are chopped finely.

Place remaining ingredients into a bowl. Add the contents of the food processor, mix well. Check for seasonings. Take squash out of the oven, dot woth butter, and stuff with the spinach mixture. You might have to really pack the stuffing in, let it mound up a little. Bake (350 degrees) for 20 minutes.

SUMMER SQUASH STUFFED WITH SESAME-SEASONED TOFU &VEGETABLES AND TAHINI SAUCE

serves 8-10

6 squash for stuffing- zucchini or yellow crookneck
1/2 lb. firm tofu, drained and crumbled
1 cup corn kernels, preferably fresh
1 medium tomato, seeded and chopped
6 slices whole wheat bread, crumbled
1/2 cup pine nuts or chopped walnuts
2 stalks celery, sliced thinly
1/2 bulb fennel, sliced very thinly
1/4 cup dark sesame oil
1 tbsp. cumin seeds
1 tsp. fennel seeds
1 tsp. (to taste) salt

Preheat oven to 350 degrees. Cut squash in half and scoop out the seeds. Place the remaining ingredients in a bowl and mix well. Stuff the squash, place them in a greased casserole dish, cover (use foil or a lid) and bake for 20 minutes. Take the cover off and bake 10 minutes more, till the top is golden brown. Serve this as is, or with a sauce, on the side. This is a good one:

Tahini Sauce
1/2 cup hot water
1 cup tahini
1 tbsp. dark miso
1 tbsp. tamari

Place all ingredients in a bowl and whisk, or in a food processor and whir. If you are serving this hot you must heat it slowly in a heavy little pot, stirring often.

SWEET CORN CHILAQUILES W/TOMATILLO SAUCE

serves 8

12 large corn-flour tortillas
2lbs. monterey jack cheese
3 cups sweet corn (fresh is best)

sauce:
3 tbsp. corn (or canola) oil
2 onions, diced
4 cloves garlic, minced
2 tbsp. cumin seeds
1 lb. fresh tomatoes, chopped
1 lb. tomatillos, husks removed and cut in quarters
1 tsp. salt
chili powder to taste

Make sauce: in a heavy pot or large skillet, heat oil. Add onions, garlic, and cumin seeds and sauté 10 minutes. Add tomatoes and tomatillos, sauté 10 minutes more. Adjust for seasonings.

To assemble the casserole: grease a 9"x13" casserole dish well. Place a layer (4 should be enough) of tortillas down, then top it with half the sauce, half the corn, and half the cheese. Put down another layer of tortillas, then the sauce, corn, and all but 1/2 cup of the cheese. Cover with foil and bake at 350 degrees for 20 minutes. Take the foil off, sprinkle on the remaining cheese and a dusting of chili powder, and bake 10 minutes more. Serve with a nice zesty salsa
and Red Chili Rice.

SWISS CHARD LEAVES STUFFED WITH HAZELNUTS AND RICE WITH BASIL SAUCE

makes 12 rolls

12 large swiss chard leaves
3 tbsp. olive oil
3 cloves garlic, minced
1 medium onion, diced fine
1 1/2 cups short-grain brown rice
1 cup mixed fresh herbs, minced: parsley, dill, oregano, and/or fennel
leaves
1 cup hazelnuts, chopped and toasted lightly
1 tsp. salt

Prepare chard leaves: cut off the bottom part of the stem. Lay the leaves in a casserole dish and pour boiling water over them. This will soften them for ease in rolling. Pour off the water after a minute or two.

Make the filling: in a heavy duty pot, heat oil and sauté the garlic and onion for 5 minutes, till they are getting brown. Add the rice and stir it around, sauteeing until it toasts lightly, about 10 minutes. Add 3 cups boiling water. Stir, cover, and lower heat. Cook 10 minutes, till rice is done. Uncover and mix in the fresh herbs, the hazelnuts, and the salt.

Make the stuffed leaves: lay a leaf in front of you, place a few spoonsful of the filling at the bottom part of the leaf, fold over the sides, and roll it up.

Set up your steamer and lay the stuffed chard leaves inside it. Steam for 15 minutes.
Serve with basil sauce:

Basil Sauce

2 cups fresh basil leaves
1 clove garlic
3 tbsp. olive oil
1 tsp. salt
1/2 cup pine nuts (or walnuts)
1 cup whole milk yogurt

Put basil, garlic, olive oil, and salt into food processor, pureé. Add nuts andyogurt, pureé till smooth. This is best served immediately but it keeps, refrigerated, for 2 days.

CURRIED RICE PILAF WITH COCONUT MILK

This side dish couldn't be easier to make, and is really, really good. A nice accompaniment to Thai or Indian cuisine.

serves 8

1 can (16 oz.) coconut milk
1 tbsp. curry powder
2 cups white jasmine or basmati rice
1 tsp. salt

In a heavy pot, bring the coconut milk and 3 cups water to a boil. Add the remaining ingredients, stir, bring to a boil again. Immediately turn off the heat, cover, and allow to steam for 15 minutes. Resist the urge to take off the lid during this time. When you finally do, you will be rewarded with a pot of nice, fluffy rice.

CURRIED TEMPEH STIR-FRY WITH RICE NOODLES

serves 4-6

1/4 cup rice vinegar
1/2 cup coconut milk
1/4 cup tamari
1 lb. tempeh, cut into 1" cubes
2 tbsp. curry powder
3 tbsp. canola oil
1 large onion, quartered and sliced thinly
3 cloves garlic, minced
1" piece of ginger, peeled and minced
1 head brocolli, cut into stir-fry-sized pieces
3 carrots, peeled and sliced
1 cup water chestnuts, sliced
1 lb. green beans, prepped for stir-fry
1 10-oz. package rice noodles

In a bowl, mix together the vinegar, the coconut milk, and the tamari. Add the tempeh and curry powder, mix well, and marinate for up to one day. Heat oil in a wok. Add the onion, garlic, and ginger, sauté 5 minutes. Add the brocolli, carrots, water chestnuts, and green beans, sauté 5 minutes. Add the tempeh with the marinade and cook over medium-high heat for 5 minutes.

Make the noodles: bring 2 quarts water to a boil. Add the noodles, bring to a boil again, turn off heat, and check to see if the noodles are cooked. They should be- if not, leave in the pot a minute or two more until they are. They should be done very quickly-don't overcook them. Drain in a colander. Add the noodles to the wok, mix well with the stir-fry over medium heat, and serve.

FETTUCINE WITH SHIITAKE MUSHROOMS AND BECHAMEL SAUCE

Is this decadent? You bet. As Adele Davis said, "...everything in moderation, including moderation..."

makes 8 servings

3 tbsp. butter
1 large white onion, chopped
4 cloves garlic, minced
1/4 cup cooking sherry
2 cups brocolli florets
1 lb. shiitake mushrooms, sliced thinly
1 tbsp. each: oregano, thyme, rosemary
1 tsp. salt
2 lbs. fettucine
fresh parsley (to garnish)

bechamel:
3 tbsp. butter
3 tbsp. flour
1 cup milk or cream
1/2 cup parmesan cheese
salt, pepper to taste

In a large skillet, melt butter and sauté onion and garlic for 5 minutes. Add sherry (or substitute water), brocolli, shiitakes, herbs, and spices. Lower heat, cover, and simmer, stirring occasionally, until the vegetables are just barely cooked, about 10 minutes. Meanwhile, cook the fettucine and drain, and...

Make the bechamel: In a small, heavy pot, melt the butter and sift in the flour. Cook over medium heat until the flour is toasty, about 5 minutes. Slowly whisk in the milk or cream, stir while cooking over medium-low heat, until it thickens. This should only take a few minutes. Stir in the parmesan and spices. simmer another 3-5 minutes, till it just starts to bubble.

To serve: In a large bowl, toss the fettucine with the bechamel until well combined, then add the sauteéd vegetables. Garnish with parsley sprigs and serve.

GINGER-BAKED (OR GRILLED) TOFU

serves 4

1 lb. tofu, drained, cut in 1/4" slices
2" piece of ginger, minced
3 tbsp. tamari
2 tbsp. sesame oil

Preheat oven to 400 degrees. Stir together the ginger, tamari, and oil. Lay the tofu on a greased baking dish. Using a pastry brush, coat both sides of the tofu slices and place in the oven. Bake for 10 minutes. Using a spatula, flip the tofu slices over and bake 10 minutes more. This is also successful when grilled.

Serve accompanied with rice and vegetables- Roasted Vegetable Medley (Chapter 1) is an especially good meal when served with this tofu dish.
Any leftovers go great in the next day's sandwich adventure.

KASHA, CARROTS, CARAWAY, & CASHEWS

Instead of bread, try serving this alongside your soup and salad repast.

serves 6

3 tbsp. olive oil
2 cloves garlic, minced
1 tbsp. caraway seeds
4 carrots, sliced thinly
1 tbsp. tamari
1 cup kasha (roasted buckwheat groats)
1/2 cup broken cashew pieces, toasted
6 scallions, sliced very thinly

In a heavy-duty pot, heat oil. Add garlic and caraway seeds, sauté 5 minutes, till the caraway seeds begin to pop. Add carrots and tamari, lower heat and cook 5 minutes. Add 2 cups water, bring to a boil, then stir in the kasha. Cover, lower heat to low, and cook 10-15 minutes, till the kasha is soft. Serve this hot or at room temperature. Before serving, stir in the cashews and half the scallions. Sprinkle the remaining scallions over the kasha and serve.

PEANUTTY-GINGERY TOFU CUTLETS

Great in sandwiches, this is a quick lunch treat.

makes 4 servings

1 lb. extra-firm tofu, drained
1 cup Curried Coconut-Peanut-Ginger Sauce (see Chapter 2)

Preheat oven to 425 degrees. Cut tofu lengthwise into squares 1/4"
thick. Lay them on a well-greased cookie sheet. Spread a dab of sauce
on each square. Bake in oven 20-25 minutes, till the tofu is slightly
browned and crisp at the edges.

PHYLLO TRIANGLES
WITH SPINACH-PINE NUT-TOFU FILLING (VEGAN)

makes 20 phyllo triangles (10 or more servings)

1 package phyllo leaves
2 lbs. spinach, rinsed and chopped
2 tbsp. canola oil
1 large onion, diced
2 cloves garlic, minced
2 lbs. extra-firm tofu, drained (squeeze out as much water as you can)
2 tbsp. dill weed
1 tsp. salt
1/2-1 cup pine nuts
up to 1 cup olive oil (for brushing the phyllo leaves)

If phyllo is frozen, take out of freezer up to 1 day, but not less than 8 hours before preparation, and place the box in the refrigerator to defrost. If you're really squeezed for time, you can defrost it out in the open for an hour but it results in less pliable dough to work with.

Steam spinach until cooked and drain thoroughly, pressing all the water out.In a heavy skillet, heat the oil and sauté the onion and garlic until it is golden, about 10 minutes. Place spinach and tofu in a food processor and pureé until it is smooth. Put this into a bowl, add the sauteédonion, the spices, and the pine nuts, and mix thoroughly. Preheat oven to 375 degrees.

Make the triangles: prepare your work area, first by taking the phyllo out of the box. Keep the olive oil and a pastry brush nearby, and place the bowl of spinach filling near you. You must work quickly now or the phyllo will dry out and become unmanageable. Lay the entire box of phyllo leaves out to one side. In front of you lay one sheet of phyllo, brush it with olive oil. Repeat this twice. Fold the phyllo into thirds (the short way). Place a couple of spoonsful of filling on the top third of the phyllo rectangle, fold the phyllo until it makes a triangle. Brush with olive oil (on both sides) and place on a greased baking sheet. Repeat this until the phyllo and/or the filling is gone. Bake for 15-20 minutes, until the triangles are golden brown.

PHYLLO TRIANGLES FILLED WITH PANEER, CHARD, AND INDIAN SPICES

Athens meets Bombay in this multi-culti culinary expression. Phyllo, that paper-thin sheet of wheat that most people associate with Greek baklava, originated in Turkey and now figures in Middle Eastern and Armenian cuisine. In this recipe it is taking the place of samosa dough as the wrapping around the filling made of Indian paneer (a soft cheese) and spices.

makes 8 servings

1 pkg. phyllo leaves
1-2 sticks (1/2-1 cup) butter, melted

filling:
3 tbsp. canola oil or butter
1" piece of ginger, minced
4 cloves garlic, minced
1 tbsp. each: cumin seeds, coriander seeds, brown mustard seeds, curry powder
2 onions, quartered and sliced thinly
1 lb. swiss chard, chopped
2 cups paneer (Indian cheese available at Indian markets; you can substitute farmer's cheese)
1 cup cashews

If the phyllo is frozen, take it out of the freezer and keep it in the refrigerator for 8 hours before you use it. If you are pressed for time, you can let out thaw out by leaving it out on the counter for an hour or two, but it's easier to use if you let it defrost slowly.

Make the filling: In a large skillet, heat oil or butter, add ginger, garlic, and spices (except curry powder) and sauté 10 minutes. Add chard and curry, lower heat, cover, and steam until the chard is cooked, about 10 minutes. Place this into a bowl with the paneer and the cashews, mix well.

Make the triangles: follow the instructions for making the Spinach-Tofu Triangles, using this filling. Use the melted butter here as you would the olive oil in that recipe. Bake for 15-20 minutes in a 325 degree oven, till golden brown.

RED CHILI RICE

This is a good base for other things. You can sauté some vegetables and add them to the rice. Top with a little sharp cheese, and call it dinner!

makes 8 servings

3 tbsp. butter or oil
1 large onion, chopped
3 cloves garlic
1 tbsp. cumin seeds
1 -3 (to taste) red chili or jalapeno peppers, minced
1 tsp. chili powder
2 cups brown rice (short, medium, or long-grain; whatever's your preference)
2 tbsp. tamari

In a heavy pot, heat oil and sauté onions, garlic, and cumin seeds 10 minutes. Add the minced pepper, chili powder, and rice, sauté 5 minutes, till the rice smells rather toasty. Pour in 1 quart hot water and the tamari, bring to a boil, lower heat, cover. Simmer 20 minutes (a little more, or a little less, depending on the type of rice you use).

SMOKED MOZZARELLA, BROWN BASMATI, AND HAZELNUT LOAF

As this involves turning on the oven for an hour, I don't make this in the summer. It's a cold-weather meal; I associate it with snow on the outside and a warm aroma floating out of the oven, inside.

makes 1 large loaf, about 8 servings

3 tbsp. canola oil
2 medium red onions, quartered and sliced thinly
2 cloves garlic, minced
1 green pepper, diced
1/2 lb. mushrooms, sliced
3 carrots, sliced thinly
2 cups brown basmati rice, cooked
3 eggs
1 cup cottage cheese
1 cup smoked mozzarella cheese, grated
1/2 cup toasted hazelnut pieces
1 tsp. each: dried oregano, thyme, fennel seeds, crushed rosemary leaves
1 tsp. salt

Heat oil in a skillet. Add onions and garlic and sauté until soft, 5 minutes. Add pepper, mushrooms, and carrots, sauté 5 minutes more; the mushrooms should be soft and the vegetables still crisp. Place the remaining ingredients into a large bowl. Add the contents of the skillet and mix well. Put this mixture into a greased loaf pan, cover with foil and bake for 1 hour (take the foil off 10 minutes before you take it out of the oven). Allow to cool for 10 minutes before you turn it (carefully) out onto a plate for serving. This is good served with a marinara tomato sauce.

SPINACH-ALMOND PILAF

serves 8

3 tbsp. olive oil
2 cloves garlic, minced
1 medium onion, chopped
2 cups brown basmati rice
1 tsp. salt
1 tbsp. dill weed
1 lb. fresh spinach, chopped
1 cup almonds, toasted and chopped

In a heavy-duty pot, heat oil. Add garlic and onions and sauté 5 minutes. Add rice and sauté 5-10 minutes, till a toasty smell emerges and the rice browns a bit. Add 1 quart hot water, the salt, dill weed, and spinach, stir. Bring to a boil, lower heat immediately to low, cover the pot and simmer 20 minutes, till the rice is done. Stir in the toasted almonds and serve.

TOASTED RICE WITH GARLIC

serves 8

2 tbsp. canola oil
5 cloves garlic, minced
1 tsp. yellow mustard seeds
2 cups white basmati rice
1 tsp. turmeric
1 tsp. salt
dash curry powder
coriander leaves, chopped (optional)

In a large heavy-duty pot, heat oil. Add garlic and sauté till garlic is golden, about 5 minutes. Add mustard seeds and sauté a minute or two more, till the seeds begin to pop (be careful, you don't want one to hit you in the eye). Immediately stir in the rice, lower heat, and sauté till the rice gets toasty, about 5 minutes. Add 4 cups boiling water, the turmeric and salt, and bring to a boil. Stir once, cover, then turn off heat. Check the pot in 15 minutes; the rice should be nice and fluffy. Sprinkle the curry powder and coriander leaves over the rice and serve.

TOFU "MEATBALLS" FOR PASTA DISHES

These are handy to have in the 'fridge waiting for you when there are better things to do than cook dinner. All you have to do is boil up some pasta, toss with sauce, and stir in these tofu "meatballs".

serves 4

1 lb. firm tofu, cut into chunks and drained
1 cup bread crumbs
1 small onion, chopped fine
2 eggs
1 tsp. each: dried oregano, thyme, garlic powder
1/2 tsp. salt

Preheat oven to 350 degrees. Place all the ingredients in a bowl and mash with a fork or your hands till well blended. Roll into balls and place on a greased baking sheet. Bake for 20-25 minutes, till golden brown. These keep, refrigerated, for a week.

Desserts

APPLE PIE WITH A DIFFERENCE

BLACKBERRY CUSTARD PIE

GINGERY SQUASH PIE- NO DAIRY

LEMON RICOTTA PIE

PEACH TART

PEAR TART WITH RASPBERRY PRESERVES

RASPBERRY-NECTARINE PIE

APPLESAUCE CAKE WITH CINNAMON ICING

BANANA-POPPYSEED CAKE

CARROT CAKE W/LEMON-CARDAMON CREAM CHEESE FROSTING

CARROT CAKE FOR A WEDDING (OR OTHER FANDANGO)

CHOCOLATE SPICE CAKE

HAZELNUT CHEESECAKE

MAPLE-SOUR CREAM CAKE WITH STREUSEL TOPPING

PINEAPPLE-GINGER UPSIDE-DOWN CAKE

SPICED APPLE CAKE

STRAWBERRY CHEESECAKE

BANANA BREAD

LEMON-POPPYSEED BREAD

HONEY SPICE MUFFINS

TOASTED ALMOND-GINGER COOKIES

OOEY GOOEY BROWNIES

OATMEAL SQUARES WITH DRIED FRUIT

CARROT HALVAH

PEARS ROLLED IN PHYLLO LEAVES

APPLE-PEAR COBBLER

Sadness and good food are incompatible.
　　　-Charles Simic

In the world of food, nothing says "I love you" more emphatically than a sweet, sumptuous dessert. It started with some of us when we were very young: mom would bake us the special cake we loved the most for our birthday; a cookie and a kiss would assuage our momentary pain of life.

In the grown-up world, sweets still have a distinct message. Pull a pie from the oven, bring it to the neighbors moving in, and you've just said "welcome". If you have a hard time knowing the right thing to say to the family who has just lost a loved one, a plate of freshly baked cookies can help say it. And then, of course, there are all those, gooey, chocolatey treats shared with amorous intent over candlelight in a quiet corner...

And holidays. Is it really a holiday without sweets? Not in my home. In fact, most of my family memories of holidays consist of the preparation, for days, before the actual event. My mother reigned as queen of desserts, and she was famous for her Hungarian pastries and breads. There was palacsinta (a crêpe filled with apricot jam), gerbeaud (shortbread pastry with walnuts and apricots), linzer torte (a raspberry-filled almond tart), and for very special occasions, there was Dobostorta. This was a 7-layer extravaganza that took most of the day to make, frosted with chocolate buttercream and topped with a layer of caramelized sugar. She and I made these things together when I was deemed old enough to. I wasn't too interested in it then, the whole cooking thing was too "girly" for my tomboy self, but I did like having an excuse to mess up the kitchen, so I stood by her side and cooked with her. I was also the only child, so I didn't have a choice. The torch of Hungarian pastry baking has been passed on to me. Do I bake these things now? No. Well, rarely. But I haven't forgotten how.

My mother raised me in that era when many women who raised children didn't work outside the home. She was a talented cook, and so, with the (what I consider) aeons of time she had on her hands, she baked extravagent, time-consuming delicacies. But that's not my life, nor is it the life of most mothers I know. We work, we raise the kids, often alone (as I have done), we don't have much time to bake. But we make the time, and we bake.

Baking sweets treats is a luxury, both in time and in ingredients. It is a private act, usually done alone (unless I am in the kitchen with my children, teaching them). I bake with the sole purpose of making the people around me, and myself, happy. And so it follows that I bake in joy. I appreciate that I have this food- flour, butter, eggs, fruit, chocolate. I have hands and a heart and a mind that has the ability to do this thing called baking. I am grateful that I have loved ones, and strangers, to bake for. And I thank you, readers of this book and eaters of the food I've prepared, to give me the opportunity to share this gift I've been given, the gift of loving and sharing food.

Cook well, cook happily.

Eat well, eat happily.

May peace be with you in the kitchen and in the world.

146

APPLE PIE WITH A DIFFERENCE

makes 1 pie, 8-10 servings

1 pie shell, unbaked
1 quart sliced apples
(use the baking apples- macoun, macintosh, granny smith, etc.)
3/4 cup honey
1 stick (1/2 cup) butter
2 cups rolled oats
1/2 cup flour (either whole wheat or white)
1 tbsp. cinnamon
1 tsp. ground ginger
1 tsp. nutmeg

Mix together the apples, honey, and half the cinnamon. Put this into the pie shell. In a saucepan, melt the butter, then stir in the remaining ingredients (and the rest of the cinnamon), mix well. Crumble this over the top of the pie. Put it in the oven and bake (350 degrees) for 30 minutes.

BLACKBERRY CUSTARD PIE

When I first came to New England, I wasn't too thrilled with the climate (too cold), until I spent a summer in the country. The roadside wild-flowers charmed and fascinated me -I memorized their names to add to my poetic vocabulary. When July and August came, I was treated to the most delicious food I'd ever had- free for the picking, along country roads- blackberries! I grow them now, but I always make sure I ride my bike along a "blackberry route" in the summer, to take advantage of the freebies. You can substitute blueberries or raspberries in this recipe, or combine the three.

makes 1 pie

the crust:
1 1/2 cups white flour
1 stick butter
1/2 tsp. ground ginger
1/2 cup grated walnuts
1/2 cup ice water

the custard:
3 eggs
2 cups milk
1 tsp. lemon extract
1 cup sugar

blackberry topping:
3 cups blackberries
1/2 cup sugar
2 tbsp. lemon juice

Make the crust: In a food processor, place flour, the butter cut into chunks, the ginger, and the walnuts. Turn on the processor and slowly drizzle in the water until it forms a solid ball that doesn't stick to the sides. Wrap in plastic and refrigerate for 1 hour.

Preheat oven to 350 degrees. Roll out dough to form a circle and place in the pie pan. Crimp the edges with a fork or your fingers. Prick the dough a few times with a fork. Lay foil on top of the dough in the pan and weight it down with pie stones- pebbles or dried beans will do. Bake 15 minutes.

Make the custard: place all custard ingredients in a small heavy saucepan and slowly heat it over medium heat, whisking it until it thickens. This should take about 10 minutes. When it's thick, pour into the pie crust. Bake at 350 degrees for 25 minutes, until the custard is set. Take the pie out and allow it to cool.

Make the topping: place the topping ingredients in a small heavy saucepan and cook for 10 minutes, till it gets syrupy. Allow to cool and pour over the pie. Chill the pie before serving.

148

GINGERY SQUASH PIE- NO DAIRY

makes 1 pie

2 cups cooked squash
1 cup honey
1/2 lb. tofu, drained
1 tsp. ground ginger
1/2 tsp. cinnamon
dash nutmeg and clove powder
1/4 cup candied ginger, minced (optional)
1 pie shell, unbaked

Place all ingredients (except pie shell and candied ginger) into a food processor and blend till very smooth. Pour into a pie shell. Sprinkle the candied ginger evenly over the pie. Bake at 350 degrees for 35-45 minutes, till the pie is golden brown.

LEMON RICOTTA PIE

Is it pie? Is it cheesecake?
Yes.

makes 1 pie
1 unbaked pie shell
4 oz. cream cheese, softened
2 eggs
1 cup sugar
1 cup ricotta cheese
2 tbsp. lemon juice
1 tbsp. grated lemon peel
1 tsp. lemon extract
1 orange, cut in half and sliced thinly (for decoration)
candied lemon slices (optional)

Preheat oven to 350 degrees. Place cream cheese, eggs, sugar, ricotta, lemon juice, lemon peel and extract into a bowl, beat well. Pour into pie shell and bake for 30 minutes, until pie is golden brown. Serve chilled or at room temperature, garnished with the orange slices and candied lemon.

PEACH TART

makes 1 tart

crust:
1 stick (1/2 cup) butter, melted
1 1/2 cups graham cracker crumbs
1/2 cup ground walnuts

filling:
8 oz. cream cheese, softened
1/4 cup vanilla yogurt
1/2 cup sugar
1 tsp. vanilla extract
3 large slightly underripe peaches, sliced thinly

Combine crust ingredients and press into the bottom and sides of a tart pan. Bake at 375 degrees for 10 minutes. Beat the cream cheese, yogurt, sugar, and vanilla till smooth. Spread this evenly in the tart shell, then artfully lay the peach slices on the top (a concentric circle is nice). Bake 30 minutes at 375 degrees. This is best when chilled before serving, but it's not bad hot, either.

PEAR TART WITH RASPBERRY PRESERVES

makes 1 large tart

cinnamon crust:
1 stick butter
1 1/4 cup unbleached white flour
1 tbsp. cinnamon
3 tbsp. sugar
up to 1/2 cup ice water

tart filling:
2 cups raspberry preserves
1 cup slivered almonds, toasted
3 large pears
(they should be firm, a little underripe), cored, halved, and sliced thinly
2 tbsp. lemon juice
1/4 cup honey

Make crust: Cut butter into chunks and put into bowl of food processor. Add remaining ingredients, except the water, and turn it on. Slowly pour in the water, stopping when the dough forms a nice solid ball. Wrap in plastic or waxed paper and refrigerate for an hour. Roll out and lay carefully in a large tart pan. Poke the crust a few times with a fork, line the pie crust with foil, and weight it with pie stones or dried beans. Bake in a preheated 425 degree oven for 10 minutes.

Make pie: When crust cools a bit (remove the foil and pie weights), spread the preserves evenly over the bottom. Toss the pear slices with the lemon juice and honey and lay them down in a concentric circle in the tart shell. Place in a 375 degree oven and bake 25 minutes.
Serve this right away, or chill it and serve it cold.

RASPBERRY-NECTARINE PIE

This is one of those pies that's equally good when it's hot out of the oven with a bit of vanilla ice cream on the side, or chilled, as a refresher on a hot summer day. Don't forget the lemonade.

makes 1 pie

1 pie shell, unbaked
1 quart fresh raspberries
2 large nectarines, sliced thinly
2 tbsp. cornstarch
1/4 cup fruit juice
1 tbsp. lemon juice
1 egg
1/2 cup sugar

Prebake pie shell 10 minutes. Mix together raspberries and nectarines. In a seperate bowl, mix cornstarch with fruit and lemon juice till smooth. Beat in egg and sugar, and stir this into the fruit mixture. Let this stand for 10 minutes. Pour into the pie shell and bake at 350 degrees for 30 minutes.

APPLESAUCE CAKE WITH CINNAMON ICING

This is a birthday cake I invented for my son who was turning 3, for his party. He was just beginning his phase of not liking anything I cooked (a phase that seemed to last 100 years but was really more like 10), but he liked this cake. So did the grown-ups who stuck around and played with their toddlers at the party.

makes 1 9"x13" sheet cake

the cake:
1 stick (1/2 cup) butter, melted
1 cup brown sugar
3 eggs
2 cups applesauce
2 tsp. baking powder
1 tsp. baking soda
2 cups unbleached white flour
1 cup whole wheat flour
2 tsp. cinnamon
1/2 tsp. nutmeg
1/2 tsp. ground cloves
1/2 tsp. ground ginger

Cream butter and sugar, beat in eggs. In another bowl, mix together the dry ingredients. Alternately add this to the batter with the applesauce, mix well, and pour into a greased and floured 9"x13" casserole dish. Bake in a preheated 350 degree oven for 35-45 minutes, until a tester comes out clean.

Meanwhile, make the icing:

icing:
2 egg whites
1 cup sugar
2 tbsp. corn syrup
1 tsp. cream of tartar
1 tbsp. cinnamon

You need a double boiler for this. Bring the water to a boil in the bottom of a double boiler, place all the ingredients in the top of it, then beat rapidly for 7-10 minutes, till the icing is thick and spreadable. When this has cooled, you can frost the cake.

BANANA-POPPYSEED CAKE

This cake is moist and tasty enough to go without frosting,
just a dusting of powdered sugar to pretty it up.

makes 1 9"x13" sheet cake

2 sticks butter
1 cup packed brown sugar
3 eggs
1 tbsp. vanilla
2 1/2 c. flour
2 tsp. baking powder
1 tsp. baking soda
2 large bananas (overripe is best)
1/2 cup milk
1/4 cup poppyseeds

Preheat oven to 350 degrees. Melt butter and beat with sugar and
vanilla. Beat in eggs, then flour, baking powder and soda. Mix well.
Mash the bananas with the milk and add to the batter, along with the
poppyseeds. Mix well, then pour into greased 9"x13" casserole dish.
Bake 40-45 minutes, till a tester comes out clean.

CARROT CAKE W/LEMON-CARDAMON CREAM CHEESE FROSTING

makes 3 9" round layers or 1 9"x13" sheet cake

cake:
1 1/2 cups (3 sticks) butter
1 cup sugar
1/2 cup honey
1 tbsp. vanilla
4 eggs
1 cup whole wheat flour
2 cups unbleached white flour
1 tbsp. cinnamon
1 tsp. nutmeg
1/2 tsp. ground ginger
1/2 tsp. ground cloves
2 tsp. baking powder
1 tsp. baking soda
3 cups grated carrots
1 cup raisins
1 cup walnuts

frosting:
1 1/2 lbs. cream cheese
1 tbsp. lemon extract
2 tsp. ground cardamon
1/2 cup honey

Preheat oven to 350 degrees. Soften butter and add sugar, honey, and vanilla, blend thoroughly. Sift together dry ingredients and alternately add this with the eggs. Stir in carrots, walnuts, and raisins. Pour batter into greased baking pan(s), bake for 35-45 minutes, till a tester comes out clean. Cool on a rack.

Make the frosting: place all the ingredients in a food processor and blend until thoroughly mixed. When the cake is cooled, frost and decorate it. Store in refrigerator till ready to serve. Any leftover frosting can be frozen for later use.

CARROT CAKE FOR A WEDDING
(OR OTHER FANDANGO)

Want to make a REALLY big cake? Here's how. You can rent big cake pans from party stores and rental supply houses. Once this cake is frosted, you don't want to move it. The best- no, the only- thing to do is frost and decorate it on the spot in which it is to be served. I make this cake for many of the weddings I cater, and because I construct it on site, people get to watch, which is fun. I decorate the cake with flowers- nasturtiums and daylilies are best (they're edible). Actually, I don't decorate it- I get the children who are attending the wedding to do it. Keeps them out of trouble for a few minutes. If you want to make a REALLY REALLY big cake, this recipe can be doubled, even tripled.

serves 75-80

5 lbs. brown sugar
6 lbs. butter, melted
30 eggs
3 quarts unbleached white flour
2 cups whole wheat flour
1/3 cup cinnamon
1/4 cup nutmeg
1/4 cup ground ginger
1/4 cup baking powder
1/4 cup baking soda
8 lbs. carrots, grated
2 lbs. broken walnut pieces
1/2 lb. pecan pieces
3 lbs. raisins

frosting:
3 lbs. cream cheese, softened
2 cups sugar
4 tsp. lemon extract
1/4 cup cardamon powder

In a large bowl, place sugar, butter, and eggs, beat well. In another large bowl, place flours, spices, baking powder and soda. In a really really big bowl, mix together the wet with the dry ingredients. Stir in the nuts, raisins, and carrots. Carefully spoon the batter into greased, floured baking pans, filling the pans halfway. Bake at 350 degrees for about least an hour, depending on how large your pans are (start testing them when they've been in the oven 45 minutes). To make the frosting, place all the ingredients into the workbowl of a food processor and mix till smooth. Frost the cake. Dance at the wedding. Kiss the bride. Kiss the groom, too.

CHOCOLATE SPICE CAKE

makes 1 10" Bundt cake

4 oz. unsweetened baking chocolate
1/2 c. milk
1 stick (1 cup) butter
2 c. sugar
3 eggs
2 c. unbleached white flour
1 1/2 tsp. baking powder
1 tsp. baking soda
1/2 tsp. each: cinnamon, cloves, nutmeg, ginger

Preheat oven to 350 degrees. In a double boiler, melt chocolate, milk, 1 c. sugar, and 1 stick (1/2 c.) butter. In a large bowl, blend the remaining butter and sugar. Seperate the eggs and add the yolks; beat well. Mix in chocolate mixture, pouring in slowly. Sift flour and add the baking powder and soda and the spices, add this to the batter. In a seperate bowl, beat the egg whites till they are frothy and peaks form. Carefully mix this into the batter, using a spatula with an over-and-under motion, and even more carefully pour this into a greased and floured Bundt pan. Bake 50 minutes, till a tester comes out clean.

I like this dusted with confectioner's sugar and a dash of cinnamon, with sliced oranges all around for decoration. Or, if you are feeling decadent, a white frosting with chocolate-covered orange slices on top is really nice.

HAZELNUT CHEESECAKE

makes 1 cheesecake

1 cup (2 sticks) butter
2 cups graham cracker crumbs
1/4 cup cocoa powder
1 1/2 cups hazelnuts
1 lb. cream cheese
3 eggs
1 lb. sour cream
1 cup confectioner's sugar
1/2 tsp. vanilla extract

Melt butter. Mix it with the cracker crumbs and the cocoa powder. Press this into the bottom of a springform cheesecake pan. Spread the hazelnuts in a baking sheet and toast them at 350 degrees until they are golden; about 10 minutes. Grind them. Place the remaining ingredients and the ground hazelnuts in a bowl and mix them with an electric mixer. Pour this into the cheesecake pan and bake in a preheated 350 degree oven for one hour.

MAPLE-SOUR CREAM CAKE WITH STREUSEL TOPPING

makes 1 10" Bundt cake

the cake:
1 stick (1/4 cup) butter or margarine, softened
1/2 cup sugar
1/2 cup maple syrup (can be the darker stuff- "b" grade)
1 tsp. vanilla extract
3 eggs
1 cup sour cream
2 1/2 cups unbleached white flour
1 tsp. baking powder
1 tsp. baking soda

streusel topping:
1 stick butter or margarine
1 1/2 cups cake crumbs
1/2 cup ground walnuts

Preheat oven to 350 degrees. In a large bowl beat butter, sugar, maple syrup, and vanilla until smooth. Add eggs and sour cream, beat well. Add flour and baking soda and powder, beat till smooth.

Make topping: In a small saucepan, melt shortening and add crumbs and walnuts, stir. This should be crumbly- if it's not, add more cake crumbs and walnuts.

Spread this evenly on the bottom of a greased and floured Bundt pan, then pour the batter in. Bake for 45-50 minutes, till a cake tester comes out clean.

PINEAPPLE-GINGER UPSIDE-DOWN CAKE

makes 1 9"x13" sheet cake

1 16-oz. can sliced pineapple
3 eggs
1 cup sugar
1 tbsp. vanilla extract
2 1/2 cups unbleached white flour
1/2 cup whole wheat flour
2 tsp. baking powder
1 tsp. baking soda
1 tsp. cinnamon
1/3 cup candied ginger, chopped fine
1 cup walnut pieces (optional)
1 cup raisins (optional)

Drain pineapple, save 8 slices, and pureé the rest. Preheat oven to 350 degrees. In a large bowl, beat the eggs, sugar, and extract. In a seperate bowl, mix together the flour, baking powder, cinnamon, and ginger. Slowly beat this into the egg mixture, then add the pureéd pineapple. Add the walnuts and raisins, if you're using them.

Grease and flour an 9"x13" casserole dish, then lay the pineapple slices on the bottom. Pour the batter in, then bake for 45-55 minutes, till a cake tester comes out clean. Serve pineapple-side up, of course; try it sprinkled with a dusting of cinnamon sugar.

SPICED APPLE CAKE

Another one that needs no frosting, but if you must, do this: put 8 oz. cream cheese and 1/2 cup maple syrup in your food processor. Mix well, and when the cake is cool, spread it on.

makes 1 9"x13" cake

1 cup (2 sticks) butter, margarine, or canola oil
1 cup sugar
1/2 cup honey
4 eggs
1 cup whole wheat flour
2 cups unbleached white flour
2 tsp. baking powder
1 tsp. baking soda
1 tsp. each: cinnamon and ground ginger
1/2 tsp. nutmeg
4 baking apples, chopped small (you can leave the peels on , if you wish)
1 cup raisins

Preheat oven to 350 degrees. Blend shortening, sugar, and honey in a large bowl. Add eggs, mix well. In a seperate bowl, mix the flours, baking powder and soda, and spices. Carefully mix this into the wet ingredients, then stir in the raisins and apples. Pour the batter into a greased, floured 9"x13" baking dish, bake for 45 minutes. Serve hot or at room temperature.

STRAWBERRY CHEESECAKE

makes 1 12" cheesecake

crust:
1 stick (1/2 c.) butter, melted
1 1/2 c. crushed graham cracker crumbs
1/2 tsp. cinnamon

filling:
1 c. strawberries, washed
1 c. sugar
1 lb. cream cheese
1 lb. ricotta cheese
2 eggs
1 c. pine nuts, toasted
garnish: more strawberries, sliced

Preheat oven to 350 degrees.
Make crust: mix the melted butter with the graham cracker crumbs
and the cinnamon, press evenly into a 12" springform pan.

Make the filling: Place strawberries in a food processor, pureé. Add
sugar, cream and ricotta cheeses and the eggs, pureé. Mix in the pine
nuts (don't pureé, just do this with a spoon, being careful not to cut
yourself on the blade. This is a bit unconventional but why use another
bowl just to mix in the pine nuts? The less dishes to wash, the better,
n'est-ce pas?) Pour this into the springform pan and bake for 45
minutes, till the top is brown. Serve at room temperature or chilled,
decorated with festive and beautiful strawberries.

A variation on this would be to do it with blueberries. Simply substitute
blueberries for strawberries and do everything the same way. You can
garnish with blueberries AND strawberries, and maybe a few more
toasted pine nuts, for good measure.

BANANA BREAD

makes 2 loaves

6-8 ripe bananas
2 eggs
1 cup honey
3/4 cup yogurt
1 stick butter or margarine, or 1/4 cup canola oil
1 1/2 cups whole wheat flour
1 1/2 cups unbleached white flour
2 tsp. baking soda
4 tsp. baking powder
1 tsp. cinnamon
1 cup walnut pieces

Preheat oven to 375 degrees. Grease 2 loaf pans. In a large bowl, mash bananas. Add eggs, honey, yogurt, and shortening. Mix well. Sift in flours, cinnamon, baking powder and baking soda. Mix well; if the batter is too runny add a little more flour. Stir in walnut pieces. Pour batter into loaf pans and bake for 50 minutes- 1 hour (top of loaves should be golden brown).

LEMON-POPPYSEED BREAD

Got kids? Are they hard to please? Make this- you'll win 'em over, for sure.

makes 2 loaves

4 eggs
2 cups light brown sugar
1 cup milk (cow or soy)
3 sticks (1 1/2 cups) butter or margarine, softened
3 cups unbleached white flour
1 tbsp. baking powder
1/2 cup poppyseeds
2 tbsp. lemon extract

Preheat oven to 350 degrees. Beat eggs till light. Add sugar, mix well. Beat in shortening, milk, then flour and baking powder. Stir in poppy-seeds and extract. Grease and flour 2 loaf pans, pour in batter, and bake for 35-45 minutes.

HONEY SPICE MUFFINS

Tired of too-sweet morning muffins? Try these.

makes 8 large muffins

1/2 cup (1 stick) butter or margarine, softened
3/4 cup honey
2 cups unbleached white flour (or 1 cup white and 1 cup whole wheat)
2 tsp. baking powder
1 tsp. baking soda
1 tsp. each: cinnamon, nutmeg, ground ginger
4 eggs
1/2 cup raisins
1 cup walnut pieces

Preheat oven to 375 degrees. Grease an 8-muffin tin (or use paper muffin tin liners, if you like). Beat together the shortening and honey. Sift together the dry ingredients and add them alternately with the eggs, until it is mixed well. Do not overbeat. Mix in the raisins and walnuts. Pour into muffin tins and bake for 25-35 minutes.

TOASTED ALMOND-GINGER COOKIES

makes about 3 dozen cookies

1 cup (2 sticks) butter or margarine, softened
1 cup packed brown sugar
2 eggs
1 cup whole wheat flour (pastry flour, if you have it)
1 cup unbleached white flour
1 tsp. baking soda
2 tsp. baking powder
2 tbsp. ground ginger
1 cup ground toasted almonds
1/2 cup candied ginger, minced
about 36 whole almonds, for garnish (optional)

Cream butter and sugar together, then beat in eggs. Sift together the flour with the remaining ingredients, except the whole almonds, and mix this into the batter. I use my hands to knead the dough, but you can use a spoon if you really want to. Place the bowl into the refrigerator and chill 1 hour.

Preheat oven to 325 degrees. Generously grease your cookie sheets. Form cookies by rolling a bit of dough in your hands and pressing the ball onto the cookie sheet, flattening it. If you are using the whole almonds, press one into the middle of each cookie. The cookies should be 1" apart on the cookie sheet.

Bake for 15-20 minutes- if you like chewy cookies, leave them in for less time, if you like them crispy, leave them in for more. Take the cookies out of the oven and place them on racks to cool (keeps 'em crispy).

OOEY GOOEY BROWNIES

makes 20 brownies

8 oz. semi-sweet baking chocolate
1/2 cup (1 stick) butter or margarine
4 eggs
1 tsp. vanilla
1 cup sugar
1 1/2 cups unbleached white flour
1 cup broken walnut pieces
1 cup white chocolate chips

Melt the chocolate and shortening over a double boiler till it is thoroughly melted. Allow to cool. (This step is very important- if you make the batter while this is still hot then the result will be a dry rather than moist brownie.) Preheat oven to 350 degrees. Whip eggs, sugar, and vanilla till fluffy. Alternately stir in the cooled chocolate mixture and the flour, beat well, and add the walnuts and the chips. Pour into a greased 9"x9" baking pan and bake for 35-40 minutes, till a tester comes out clean.

OATMEAL SQUARES WITH DRIED FRUIT

makes 12 bars

1 lb. dried fruit (a combination of any or all of these: raisins, currants,
cranberries, pitted prunes, apricots, apples)
1 cup orange juice
2 sticks butter, softened
1/2 c. whole wheat flour
1/2 c. unbleached white flour
2 cups rolled oats
1 tbsp. cinnamon
1 cup sugar

Preheat oven to 350 degrees. In a small heavy pot, simmer dried fruit
and orange juice 20 minutes, until the juice is almost gone. Place the
remaining ingredients in a bowl and mix with your hands until it is
thoroughly blended.

Grease a 8"x8" casserole dish and press 1/2 the dough evenly into it.
Spread the fruit mixture on this. Top with the remaining dough,
smoothing it out as well as possible, and bake for 40 minutes.
Cool and slice into bars.

CARROT HALVAH

A sweet finale to an Indian repast. Making halvah requires the maker to stand at the stove and stir the pot nonstop for almost an hour. Make it fun by bringing in the boombox. If you love to dance, and you love to cook, it doesn't get better than this.

makes 40 pieces

2 sticks butter
2 lbs. ricotta cheese
12-oz. can evaporated milk
8 cups grated carrots
1 cup honey
1 tsp. ground cardamon
2 tbsps. fennel seeds
1 tbsp. cardamon seeds
1 cup shelled pistachios

In a large heavy pot, melt 1 1/2 sticks butter, add ricotta and milk. Simmer over medium heat, stirring frequently. Add carrots, honey, and ground cardamon, and cook over medium-low heat for 45 minutes, stirring constantly. While you are doing this, melt the remaining butter in a small skillet and add the fennel and cardamon seeds, cook over high heat a minute ir two, till the seeds are brown and begin to pop. Lower heat immediately and add the pistachios, toasting them for 5 minutes.

Keep stirring the carrot mixture and when it is very thick, like a dough, stir in the sauteéd nuts and seeds. Turn off the heat. Grease a small cookie sheet or casserole pan and pour the halvah into it. Press down firmly and evenly. Chill.

When halvah is cold, cut into very small squares- this is a rich dessert. It keeps, wrapped and refrigerated, for several weeks.

PEARS ROLLED IN PHYLLO LEAVES

makes 5 8" rolls

8 large Bartlett pears, cored and sliced thinly
1/2 cup sugar
1 cup raisins
1 cup shredded sweetened coconut
1 tsp. cinnamon
1/2 tsp. nutmeg
1 cup sliced almonds
1 cup (2 sticks) butter
1 box phyllo dough, thawed

Preheat oven to 350 degrees. Mix pears with all ingredients, except the butter and phyllo. Melt butter.

Prepare your workspace: place melted butter (with a pastry brush) and pear mixture to one side of a cleared tabletop or counter. Open the box of phyllo, take it out of its plastic package, and unfold it. Lifting up one layer at a time, lay a leaf of phyllo in front of you and brush it with butter. Repeat this 7 times.

Spoon out 1/5 of the pear mixture in a line along the center, long ways. Fold over the edges, then roll the phyllo jellyroll-fashion, brushing the edges with
butter to seal. Generously brush the top with butter. Carefully place this on a greased baking sheet.

Make 4 more rolls this way, and place the baking sheets in the oven. Bake for 20 minutes, until the top is golden. Slice it when you are ready to serve. Serve hot or at room temperature.

APPLE-PEAR COBBLER

You can use all apples and omit the pears, if you like.
This is a great, user-friendly dessert, not fussy at all to make.

serves 10-12

1 1/2-2 quarts apple and Bartlett pear slices (slightly underripe pears
are best)
2 tbsp. cinnamon
2 tbsp. lemon juice
1 cup chopped walnuts (optional)
2 sticks (1 cup) butter, melted
1 1/2 cups rolled (old-fashioned) oats
1/2 cup whole wheat flour
1/2 cup honey
1/2 cup brown sugar
1 tsp. nutmeg
1 tsp. ground ginger

Preheat oven to 350 degrees. Grease a 9"x13" casserole dish. In a large
bowl, stir the fruit slices, 1 tbsp. cinnamon, the lemon juice, and the
walnuts, if you're using them. Pour this into the casserole dish. Mix
together the remaining cinnamon and the rest of the ingredients until it
is crumbly (if it's too wet, add some more flour). Spread this evenly over
the top of the fruit slices, put into the oven, and bake for 30-40
minutes, till the top is golden brown.

Serve hot, with ice cream or whipped cream, if you wish. This isn't bad
for breakfast the next day, either; it's good cold or at room temperature.

NIGHT KITCHEN

never trust an artichoke
it protects its heart
so cautiously

potatoes revel in disguises

yellow food is friendly-
broad smile of squash,
lemons never without a pleasantry

-beware the ginger and the garlic-

rice is patient:
thousands of years of oriental
feet wrinkled like raisins
planting in the paddies

yeast conjures up the dough

mushrooms marinate
as I wait
for you

GRATITUDE

There are many people whom I have not met who have inspired, taught, and fed both my body and my soul. Though they don't know me, I know them; I hope to show my gratitude for what I've received from them by trying mightily to give away what has been so generously given to me. The stream of life flows through me to the sentient and non-sentient beings of this world.

I would also like to thank the good people at the Providence Zen Center, where I am invited to bring my "don't know" mind into the kitchen. Many thanks to Steve Scanlon, without whose help this book would still be in its bardo state in my computer. And thanks to my family- to my sons, Nick and Jeremy, and to the love of my life, Tim.

ABOUT THE AUTHOR

Karen Bard was born in Washington, D.C., and grew up in Alexandria, VA. She attended Carnegie-Mellon and George Washington Universities for a B.F.A., and recieved an M.A. from Brown University in Creative Writing. She is a landscape photographer and writer of poetry; she has exhibited her photography in galleries in New England and Virginia and published her poetry in numerous literary magazines. For the past 16 years she has lived in a 300-year-old house in rural northeast Connecticut with her two sons. She is a professional vegetarian cook and caterer. For professional inquiries she can be reached at 860-928-5896.